Better Homes and Gardens®

COOKIES
for
Christmas

Our seal assures you that every recipe in *Cookies for Christmas* has been tested in the Better Homes and Gardens® Test Kitchen. This means that each recipe is practical and reliable, and meets our high standards of taste appeal.

BETTER HOMES AND GARDENS® BOOKS
Editor: Gerald M. Knox
Art Director: Ernest Shelton
Managing Editor: David A. Kirchner
Copy and Production Editors: Marsha Jahns, Mary Helen Schiltz,
    Carl Voss, David A. Walsh

Food and Nutrition Editor: Nancy Byal
Department Head—Cook Books: Sharyl Heiken
Associate Department Heads: Sandra Granseth,
    Rosemary C. Hutchinson, Elizabeth Woolever
Senior Food Editors: Julia Malloy, Marcia Stanley, Joyce Trollope
Associate Food Editors: Barbara Atkins, Linda Foley, Linda Henry,
    Lynn Hoppe, Jill Johnson, Mary Jo Plutt, Maureen Powers,
    Martha Schiel
Recipe Development Editor: Marion Viall
Test Kitchen Director: Sharon Stilwell
Test Kitchen Photo Studio Director: Janet Pittman
Test Kitchen Home Economists: Jean Brekke, Kay Cargill,
    Marilyn Cornelius, Jennifer Darling, Maryellyn Krantz,
    Lynelle Munn, Dianna Nolin, Marge Steenson, Cynthia Volcko

Associate Art Directors: Linda Ford Vermie, Neoma Alt West,
    Randall Yontz
Assistant Art Directors: Lynda Haupert, Harijs Priekulis,
    Tom Wegner
Senior Graphic Designers: Mike Eagleton, Lyne Neymeyer,
    Stan Sams
Graphic Designers: Mike Burns, Sally Cooper,
    Darla Whipple-Frain, Brian Wignall

Vice President, Editorial Director: Doris Eby
Executive Director, Editorial Services: Duane L. Gregg

Senior Vice President, General Manager: Fred Stines
Director of Publishing: Robert B. Nelson
Vice President, Retail Marketing: Jamie Martin
Vice President, Direct Marketing: Arthur Heydendael

COOKIES FOR CHRISTMAS
Editor: Jill Johnson
Copy and Production Editor: Marsha Jahns
Graphic Designer: Randall Yontz
Electronic Text Processor: Joyce Wasson
Contributing Photographers: Wm. Hopkins, Scott Little,
    William K. Sladcik, Inc.
Food Stylists: Janet Pittman, Bonnie Rabert

On the front cover:
Rolled Sugar Cookies and Candy Window Sugar Cookies (page 42)
Tiny Holiday Tarts with Almond-Raspberry Filling (page 92)
Pan Lebkuchen (page 64)
Gingerbread Teddy Bears (page 21)
Cinnamon Stars (page 89)
Candy Canes (page 22)
Tiny Gingerbread Town Church (page 48)

Each of us has a different idea of the kinds of cookies that should appear on the Christmas cookie platter. We always seem to expect what our mothers and grandmothers made for us. Spritz cookies have always been my favorite because my mom made them every year without fail. She also made delicious meringue cookies with chocolate chips in them, which we kids lovingly called "balsa wood cookies" because they were so lightweight.

Some traditions are worth hanging on to and others can be modified or exchanged for new ones as our tastes change. The pages of this book are filled with that discriminating blend of old and new. For example, Spritz will always be Spritz. But the turtledoves on page 90 are actually an updated version of my childhood "balsa wood cookies."

To give you a peek at the kinds of cookies the rest of our food staff bakes at Christmas, I asked our food editors and home economists to share with you the recipes they've grown especially fond of over the years. You'll see the words "Editor's Favorite" by the titles of these recipes. Already I've adopted one of them, Scandinavian Almond Bars, as a new favorite of my own, and undoubtedly it will become a tradition in my family.

Mom, they're *almost* as good as your Spritz.

Jill Johnson

GET IN THE CHRISTMAS SPIRIT   6

Lots of cookie ideas to put you in a merry mood, including making cookie ornaments, giving cookie gifts, hosting a cookie swap, and streamlining your baking.

SHAPED COOKIES   11

Cookie creations lovingly molded by hand or shaped with the help of specialty utensils.

CUTOUT COOKIES   37

Rolling pin productions cut out with cookie cutters or with a knife.

BAR COOKIES   57

One-pan baking that gives you lots of cookies with little time and effort.

DROP COOKIES 71

Stir-and-drop doughs that bake into crispy, chewy, or cakey delights.

SLICED COOKIES 81

Refrigerated rolls of dough that you slice and bake for make-ahead convenience.

MACAROONS, MERINGUES, & TARTLETS 87

A potpourri presenting two types of featherweight cookies along with miniature filled tarts.

INDEX 94

Get in the Christmas Spirit

When the calendar flips to December and the sights, sounds, and smells of Christmas start to appear, what better way to inaugurate the season than to bake Christmas cookies?

There's no single definition of Christmas cookies. They may be cookies you bake year after year as part of family tradition, or a new recipe to try for holiday guests. They might be rich and delectable, reflecting the goodwill of the season.

Possibly the way they're decorated makes them Christmas cookies. Or maybe you've used Christmastime ingredients such as nuts, spices, candied fruit, or mincemeat. Whatever your definition, you'll find that baking a batch of cookies will quickly get you in the Christmas spirit.

Swirled Mint Cookies (page 23)

Old-Fashioned Sugar Cookies (page 44)

Scandinavian Almond Bars (page 63)

Snowmen (page 31)

Candy Window Sugar Cookies (page 42)

Pealing Bells (page 84)

Pizzelles (page 34)

Meringue Turtledoves (page 90)

Tiny Holiday Tarts (page 92)

Rolled Sugar Cookies (page 42)

Spritz (page 36)

Making Cookie Ornaments

The custom of hanging cookies on trees has been popular for generations in both German and Swedish cultures. Turning your Christmas cookies into tree ornaments is a simple matter. Cutout cookies or other flat, sturdy cookies work best for this.

Before you bake, use a drinking straw to poke a hole in the top end of each cookie. If you notice when taking the cookies out of the oven that the holes have sealed up too much to allow a string to pass through, make the holes again while the cookies are still soft.

Cool the cookies well and frost them, if you like. Let the frosting dry till firm. Then run ribbon, yarn, or thread through the holes in the cookies. Tie the ribbon at the top, forming a loop large enough for hanging on a tree branch.

Giving Cookie Gifts

Early American families learned to make Christmas cookies "by the washbasketful" so they would have plenty to give to neighbors as thanks for borrowed cookie cutters. Giving away cookies as gifts is part of the fun of making them. And part of the fun of giving cookies is packaging them in a clever and appealing way.

Containers can be as simple or as fancy as you want to make them. Ribbontied paper sacks or gussied up coffee cans or shortening cans are some of the simplest homemade carriers for cookies. Another is a large wide-mouth canning jar that shows off the cookies well. Cover the lid with a pinked square of fabric and secure it by screwing on the outer metal ring.

Here's a novel idea. Display your cookies in plastic fruit or vegetable baskets that you get in the produce department. Line the basket with cellophane and weave a ribbon through the holes in the basket to give it a festive look.

Gift shops are stocking lots of clever cardboard containers printed with holiday graphics. These make delightful and often reusable gift packages. And don't overlook the ever-popular cookie tin for giving away cookies.

Whatever the outside container, be sure the cookies inside are well protected from air and moisture. Even the most attractively packaged cookies will be a disappointment if they taste stale. If the container you're using does not have a tight-fitting lid, wrap the cookies in plastic wrap or seal them in a plastic bag before placing in the container.

Mailing Christmas Cookies

Nothing spreads cheer across the miles like a box full of homemade Christmas cookies. Make sure the contents of your package are received in the condition they were sent by heeding some simple packing tips.

Holidays are the busiest mailing times, so ask your local post office or parcel service when packages need to be sent to arrive on time.

Choose cookies that travel well. Most bar cookies are

good senders, as are soft, moist drop cookies. Frosted and filled cookies are not good choices because the frosting or filling may soften, causing the cookies to stick to one another or to the wrapping. If you want to send cutout cookies, send those with rounded edges instead of those with points that break off easily.

Find a heavy box for sending cookies. Line it with plastic wrap or foil. Lay down a generous layer of filler such as bubble wrap, foam packing pieces, or crumpled tissue paper, waxed paper, or brown paper bags.

Wrap cookies in pairs, back to back, or individually with plastic wrap. Using the sturdiest cookies on the bottom, place a single layer of wrapped cookies on top of the base filler. Top with a layer of filler. Continue layering, ending with plenty of filler (see cutaway box at left). The box should be full enough to prevent shifting of its contents when closed.

For added protection, as well as good looks, first layer cookies and waxed paper in a cookie tin or decorative coffee or shortening can with a reclosable plastic lid. Then pack this container in a well-padded box for shipping.

Before closing the box of cookies, insert a card with the addresses of both sender and receiver in case the box is accidentally torn open. Tape the box shut with strapping tape containing reinforcing fibers. Masking and cellophane tapes may crack, tear, or pull away from the package with exposure to cold and moisture. Avoid using paper overwraps and string, which may get torn off or caught in automatic equipment.

Address the box and apply transparent tape over the address to keep it from becoming smeared or blurred from moisture or handling. Mark the box "perishable" to encourage careful handling.

Host a Cookie Swap

Norwegians say there must be a different kind of cookie for each day of the Christmas season. If a variety of cookies is a part of your Christmas tradition, hold a cookie swap and get many kinds of cookies with the effort of making one.

Rally four to 10 friends, keeping in mind that the more involved, the more unwieldy the event can become and the more cookies each will have to bake.

Decide on a place and date. Ask each person to bring one dozen cookies for *each* participant, including himself or herself, plus a few extra for the "tasting plate."

Have everyone bring an empty container for taking cookies home. All containers and lids should be marked with the owner's name to prevent a mix-up.

If you and your friends like to share recipes, ask them to bring copies of their cookie recipe, too.

Have a long table or counter ready at the swap where containers can be placed as guests arrive. Divide each person's cookies among the empty containers, as well as the "tasting plate." Then set out the plate for all to enjoy.

Kids in the Kitchen

Kids love to help bake cookies. Let them mix and shape dough with their hands, roll out and cut out dough, drop dough from a spoon onto a cookie sheet, and decorate with colored sugars, candies, and icings.

Adults should always supervise difficult or hazardous steps such as beating with an electric mixer, transferring cookie sheets to or from a hot oven, and chopping nuts.

Baking in Progress

Here are a few tips to help your cookie baking run smoothly.
● Read the entire recipe before you start, then follow it exactly.
● Beat butter or margarine with an electric mixer on *medium* speed about 30 seconds to soften it. Using high speed may sling the butter out of the bowl and

low speed can burn out the motor of your mixer.
● For stiff doughs, beat in flour with a full-size electric mixer or stir it in by hand.
● To firm up doughs for easier handling, form the dough into a flat loaf, cover or wrap with clear plastic wrap, and chill in the refrigerator till firm. For a really quick chill, place the dough in the freezer for one-third the time you would refrigerate it.
● One way to simplify baking is to make up the dough and chill it for up to one week (except for thin batters and meringue-type doughs). All that's left is the baking, on the day you choose. If you find the chilled dough has become too firm to work with, let it stand at room temperature to soften.
● Preheat the oven about 10 minutes before baking.
● Always place cookie dough on cool cookie sheets to keep it from spreading.
● As a rule, place cookies that contain leavening 2 inches apart on cookie sheets. Place unleavened cookies 1 to 1½ inches apart.
● Bake on the middle oven rack for even baking.
● Remove cookies from cookie sheets immediately unless otherwise directed in recipes.
● Cool cookies on a rack for air circulation. Wire racks are best because they are washed easily. Wooden racks may get spotted from the oils in cookies.

Storing Cookies

To protect cookies from air and humidity that can make them stale, keep them in tightly covered containers. Store bar cookies this way or in the baking pan, tightly covered with plastic wrap or foil. Store moist and crisp cookies separately to avoid softening the crisp ones.

To restore moisture to soft cookies that have begun to dry out, place a wedge of raw apple or a slice of bread

underlined with waxed paper into the container with the cookies and seal tightly. Remove the apple or bread after 24 hours.

For long-term storage, freeze baked cookies in freezer containers or plastic bags for up to 12 months. Before serving, thaw them in the container or plastic.

Bulk dough, with the exception of meringue-type dough, can be frozen for baking later. Store the dough in freezer containers for up to six months. Before baking, thaw it in the container.

SHAPED COOKIES

Like snowflakes, cookies are created in all sorts of shapes. Use your hands to form the dough into balls, logs, crescents, wreaths, candy canes, snowmen, and even teddy bears. Or create fanciful cookies such as Spritz, Pizzelles, and Krumkake with the help of special equipment.

Making Dough Easy to Handle

Balls, ropes, logs, and other cookies shaped by hand need to be made from doughs that are firm enough to handle without sticking to your fingers. You can shape some cookies, such as Sandies, right after you mix them. Other cookies need chilling to firm them up for handling. If a dough needs to be chilled, work with only a small amount of dough and keep the rest chilled so it will be firm when you're ready to work with it. (See page 10, Baking in Progress.)

Flattening Dough

Try several techniques for flattening balls of dough on a cookie sheet.

● One of the easiest ways to flatten dough is with the bottom of a glass. First press the bottom of the glass into the cookie dough so that sugar will stick to it. Then dip the glass in sugar and press down gently on the ball of dough. The sugar will keep the glass from sticking to each cookie. Colored sugar or cinnamon-sugar adds interest to light-colored cookies.

● Use a fork as another tool to flatten balls of dough. Press the tines into the dough on the cookie sheet in one direction. To make a crisscross pattern, press again with the tines going another direction.

● Ceramic or wooden cookie stamps flatten and leave a design in the dough at the same time. Lightly flour the stamp before pressing down on the ball of dough. A glass with an attractive design in the bottom gives a similar effect.

When Are They Done?

Bake hand-shaped balls, flattened balls, ropes, logs, and cookie-press cookies until the edges of the cookies are firm and the bottoms are light golden brown. Thin cookies that you roll up or shape after baking are done when the edges are lightly browned. Bake cookies that require special equipment according to the manufacturer's directions.

Sandies

Several of our food editors claimed these buttery classics as their favorite Christmas cookies.

1 cup butter *or* margarine
⅓ cup sugar
2 teaspoons water
2 teaspoons vanilla
2¼ cups all-purpose flour
1 cup chopped pecans
¼ cup powdered sugar

● In a large mixer bowl beat butter or margarine till softened. Add sugar and beat till fluffy. Add water and vanilla and beat well. Stir in flour and nuts.

● Shape into 1-inch balls or 1½x½-inch fingers. Place on an ungreased cookie sheet. Bake in a 325° oven about 20 minutes or till done. Remove and cool. In a plastic bag gently shake a few at a time in powdered sugar. Makes about 45.

Gingersnaps

Spicy, crisp, and old-fashioned enough to be respected.

2¼ cups all-purpose flour
2 teaspoons baking soda
1 teaspoon ground ginger
1 teaspoon ground cinnamon
½ teaspoon ground cloves
¼ teaspoon salt
1 cup packed brown sugar
¾ cup shortening *or* cooking oil
¼ cup molasses
1 egg
Sugar (optional)

● Stir together flour, baking soda, ginger, cinnamon, cloves, and salt. In a large mixer bowl combine brown sugar, shortening or cooking oil, molasses, and egg. Beat well. Add flour mixture and beat till well mixed.

● Shape the dough into 1-inch balls. Roll in sugar, if desired. Place 2 inches apart on an ungreased cookie sheet. Bake in a 375° oven about 10 minutes or till done. Remove and cool. Makes about 48.

Pistachio Wreaths

You'll find the dough very easy to work with—not sticky or stiff.

　2　cups all-purpose flour
　¼　teaspoon baking powder
　¼　teaspoon salt
　¾　cup butter *or* margarine
　¾　cup sugar
　1　egg
　½　teaspoon vanilla
　½　teaspoon almond extract
　¼　teaspoon green food
　　　coloring
　¼　cup coarsely chopped
　　　pistachios

● Stir together flour, baking powder, and salt. In a large mixer bowl beat butter or margarine till softened. Add sugar and beat till fluffy. Add egg, vanilla, and almond extract and beat well.

● Add flour mixture and beat till well mixed. Divide the dough in half. Stir food coloring into one half. Cover each half and chill at least 30 minutes or till easy to handle.

● On a lightly floured surface, shape about one-half of a measuring tablespoon of plain dough into a 6-inch rope. Repeat with about ½ tablespoon of green dough. Place ropes side by side and twist together about six times. Form twisted ropes into a circle, gently pinching where ends meet. Place on an ungreased cookie sheet.

● Repeat with remaining dough, leaving 2 inches between cookies. Place a small amount of pistachios in one spot on each wreath. Bake in a 375° oven about 10 minutes or till done. Cool on cookie sheet about 1 minute, then remove and cool thoroughly. Makes about 24.

Poinsettia Balls

Red-petaled nut balls with a hint of orange and spice.

1½　cups all-purpose flour
　¼　teaspoon baking soda
　¼　teaspoon salt
　¼　teaspoon ground nutmeg
　½　cup butter *or* margarine
　⅓　cup honey
　1　egg yolk
1½　teaspoons finely shredded
　　　orange peel
　4　teaspoons orange juice
　1　slightly beaten egg white
　1　cup finely chopped pecans
　½　cup red candied cherries
　　　(3 ounces)

● Stir together flour, baking soda, salt, and nutmeg. In a small mixer bowl beat butter or margarine till softened. Beat in honey. Add egg yolk, orange peel, and orange juice and beat well. Add flour mixture and beat till well mixed. Cover and chill at least 3 hours or till easy to handle.

● Shape into 1-inch balls. Dip in egg white, then roll in nuts. Place 2 inches apart on an ungreased cookie sheet. Cut each cherry into six to eight petals. Place four or five petals on top of each ball and press lightly. Bake in a 325° oven for 15 to 18 minutes or till done. Remove and cool. Makes about 36.

Poinsettia Balls

Pistachio Wreaths

Hazelnut Snaps
(see recipe, page 32)

Lemon-Coriander Crescents

The lemony flavor of coriander enhances the fresh lemon taste of these tender cookies.

¾ cup butter *or* margarine
⅓ cup sifted powdered sugar
¼ teaspoon finely shredded
    lemon peel
1 tablespoon lemon juice
1 teaspoon ground coriander
2 cups all-purpose flour
⅓ cup powdered sugar

● In a large mixer bowl beat butter or margarine till softened. Add ⅓ cup sifted powdered sugar and beat till fluffy. Add lemon peel, lemon juice, and coriander and beat well. Add flour and beat till well mixed.

● Shape into 1½x½-inch logs. Curve each into a crescent moon shape, tapering the ends. Place on an ungreased cookie sheet. Bake in a 325° oven for 18 to 20 minutes or till done. Remove and cool. In a plastic bag gently shake a few cookies at a time in ⅓ cup powdered sugar. Makes about 48.

Molasses Butterballs

An old favorite, Sandies, takes on a new taste when you add brown sugar and molasses.

1 cup butter *or* margarine
¼ cup packed brown sugar
¼ cup molasses
2¼ cups all-purpose flour
2 cups very finely chopped
    walnuts
½ cup powdered sugar

● In a large mixer bowl beat butter or margarine till softened. Add brown sugar and molasses and beat till fluffy. Add flour and beat till well mixed. Stir in nuts.

● Shape dough into 1-inch balls. Place on an ungreased cookie sheet. Bake in a 325° oven about 20 minutes or till done. Remove and cool. In a plastic bag gently shake a few at a time in powdered sugar. Makes about 56.

Chocolate Mint Creams

Here's a tip from the editor who submitted this recipe as her favorite: You can find the mints for these cookies at candy shops, department store candy counters, or food gift shops.

1¼ cups all-purpose flour
½ teaspoon baking soda
⅔ cup packed brown sugar
6 tablespoons butter *or* margarine
1 tablespoon water
1 6-ounce package (1 cup) semisweet chocolate pieces
1 egg
½ to ¾ pound pastel cream mint kisses

● Stir together flour and baking soda. In a medium saucepan heat and stir brown sugar, butter or margarine, and water over low heat till butter is melted. Add chocolate pieces. Heat and stir till chocolate is melted. Pour into a large mixing bowl and let stand for 10 to 15 minutes or till cool.

● Beat egg into chocolate mixture. Stir in the flour mixture till well mixed. (Dough will be soft.) Cover and chill for 1 to 2 hours or till easy to handle.

● Shape into 1-inch balls. Place 2 inches apart on an ungreased cookie sheet. Bake in a 350° oven for 8 minutes. Remove and immediately top each cookie with a mint. Return to the oven and bake about 2 minutes more or till cookies are done. Swirl the melted mints with a knife to "frost" cookies. Remove and cool till mints are firm. Makes about 48.

"Frosting" the cookies
Bake the cookies till they're almost done. Top each with a candy mint and put the cookies back in the oven till done. The mints will melt so that you can spread them over the tops of the cookies like frosting.

Meltaways

Buttery melt-in-your-mouth cookies topped off with browned butter frosting.

¾ cup butter *or* margarine
½ cup packed brown sugar
1 egg yolk
1½ teaspoons vanilla
2 cups all-purpose flour
   Sugar
   Browned Butter Frosting
¼ to ⅓ cup chopped pecans
   (optional)

● In a large mixer bowl beat butter or margarine till softened. Add brown sugar and beat till fluffy. Add egg yolk and vanilla and beat well. Add flour and beat till well mixed. Cover and chill at least 2 hours or till easy to handle.

● Shape into 1-inch balls. Place 2 inches apart on an ungreased cookie sheet. Flatten with the bottom of a glass dipped in sugar. Bake in a 350° oven for 7 to 9 minutes or till done. Remove and cool. Frost with Browned Butter Frosting and, if desired, sprinkle with pecans, gently pressing nuts into frosting. Makes about 42.

Browned Butter Frosting: In a saucepan heat ¼ cup *butter or margarine* over low heat till lightly browned. Remove from heat. Stir in 2¼ cups sifted *powdered sugar,* 1 teaspoon *vanilla,* and enough *milk* (2 to 3 tablespoons) to make frosting spreadable.

Finnish Chestnut Fingers

To harden the chocolate faster, chill the dipped cookies in the refrigerator for 5 to 10 minutes.

1 cup all-purpose flour
¼ teaspoon salt
¼ teaspoon ground cinnamon
6 tablespoons butter *or* margarine
¼ cup sugar
1 egg yolk
½ cup chestnut puree *or* 6 ounces canned vacuum-packed chestnuts, drained and pureed
½ teaspoon vanilla
3 squares (3 ounces) semisweet chocolate *or* ½ cup semisweet chocolate pieces

● Stir together flour, salt, and cinnamon. In a small mixer bowl beat butter or margarine till softened. Add sugar and beat till fluffy. Add egg yolk and beat well. Beat in chestnut puree and vanilla. Add flour mixture and beat till well mixed.

● Using a scant tablespoon of dough for each cookie, shape into 2½x½-inch fingers. Place on a greased cookie sheet. Sprinkle with additional sugar. Bake in a 350° oven about 20 minutes or till done. Remove and cool.

● Meanwhile, in a heavy small saucepan heat chocolate over low heat till melted, stirring constantly. When cookies are cool, dip one end of each in the melted chocolate. Place on waxed paper and cool till chocolate is set. Makes about 30.

Cream Cheese Snowcaps

Snowballs of dough melt into mounded snowcaps as they bake.

1 cup all-purpose flour
1½ teaspoons baking powder
½ cup butter *or* margarine
1 3-ounce package cream
  cheese
½ cup sugar
¼ teaspoon lemon *or*
  almond extract
1 cup powdered sugar

● Combine flour and baking powder. In a small mixer bowl beat butter or margarine and cream cheese till softened. Add sugar and extract and beat till fluffy. Add flour mixture and beat till well mixed. Cover and chill for 1 to 2 hours or till easy to handle.

● Shape into 1-inch balls. Place on an ungreased cookie sheet. Bake in a 350° oven for 12 to 15 minutes or till done. Remove and cool slightly. In a plastic bag gently shake a few cookies at a time in powdered sugar. Cool thoroughly. When cool, shake cookies again in powdered sugar. Makes about 36.

Eggnog Thumbprints

Fill each thumbprint with a pool of rum-flavored cream and then sprinkle with nutmeg.

¾ cup butter *or* margarine
½ cup sugar
¼ cup packed brown sugar
1 egg
½ teaspoon vanilla
¼ teaspoon salt
2 cups all-purpose flour
¼ cup butter *or* margarine
1 cup sifted powdered sugar
1 tablespoon rum*
  Ground nutmeg

● In a large mixer bowl beat ¾ cup butter or margarine till softened. Add sugar and brown sugar and beat till fluffy. Add egg, vanilla, and salt and beat well. Add flour and beat till well mixed. Cover and chill about 1 hour or till easy to handle.

● Shape into 1-inch balls. Place 2 inches apart on an ungreased cookie sheet. Press down centers with thumb. Bake in a 350° oven about 12 minutes or till done. Remove and cool.

● For filling, in a small mixer bowl beat ¼ cup butter or margarine till softened. Add powdered sugar and beat till fluffy. Add rum and beat well. Spoon about ½ teaspoon filling into center of each cookie. Sprinkle with nutmeg. Chill till filling is firm. Makes about 50.

*You may substitute 1 tablespoon *milk* and ¼ teaspoon *rum extract* for the rum.

Gingerbread Teddy Bears

Candy Canes
(see recipe, page 22)

Peppernuts

Gingerbread Teddy Bears

Jolly ginger teddies have crisp outsides and soft, chewy insides. (Also pictured on the cover.)

1 cup butter *or* margarine
⅔ cup packed brown sugar
⅔ cup dark corn syrup, light
    corn syrup, *or* molasses
4 cups all-purpose flour
1½ teaspoons ground cinnamon
1 teaspoon ground ginger
¾ teaspoon baking soda
½ teaspoon ground cloves
1 beaten egg
1½ teaspoons vanilla
    Miniature semisweet
      chocolate pieces
    Decorating Icing (optional)

● In a saucepan combine butter, brown sugar, and corn syrup. Cook and stir over medium heat till butter is melted and sugar is dissolved. Pour into a large mixing bowl and cool 5 minutes. Meanwhile, combine flour, cinnamon, ginger, soda, and cloves.

● Add egg and vanilla to butter mixture and mix well. Add the flour mixture and beat till well mixed. Divide the dough in half. Cover and chill at least 2 hours or overnight.

● To make each teddy bear, shape dough into one 1-inch ball, one ¾-inch ball, six ½-inch balls, and five ¼-inch balls. On an ungreased cookie sheet flatten the 1-inch ball to ½ inch for body. Attach the ¾-inch ball for head and flatten to ½ inch. Attach the ½-inch balls for arms, legs, and ears. Place one of the ¼-inch balls on head for nose. Arrange remaining ¼-inch balls atop ends of arms and legs for paws. Use miniature chocolate pieces for eyes and navel.

● Bake in a 350° oven for 8 to 10 minutes or till done. Carefully remove and cool. If desired, pipe on bow ties with Decorating Icing. Makes 16.

Decorating Icing: Combine ½ cup sifted *powdered sugar* and enough *milk or light cream* (about 2 teaspoons) to make of piping consistency. Tint with one or two drops *food coloring.*

Peppernuts

These spicy nuggets are about as big as the tip of your little finger. Once you start munching, it's hard to stop.

¾ cup sugar
⅔ cup dark corn syrup
¼ cup milk
¼ cup shortening
1 teaspoon anise extract
½ teaspoon baking powder
½ teaspoon vanilla
¼ teaspoon salt
¼ teaspoon ground cinnamon
¼ teaspoon ground cardamom
¼ teaspoon ground cloves
3⅓ cups all-purpose flour
    Sifted powdered sugar

● In a large saucepan combine sugar, corn syrup, milk, and shortening. Bring to boiling. Remove from heat and cool about 15 minutes. Stir in anise extract, baking powder, vanilla, salt, cinnamon, cardamom, and cloves. Stir in the flour till well mixed. Cover and chill about 2 hours or till easy to handle.

● Divide dough into 24 equal parts. On a surface dusted lightly with sifted powdered sugar, roll each part of the dough into a ¼-inch-thick rope. Cut into pieces about ⅜ inch long. Place 1 inch apart on a greased cookie sheet.

● Bake in a 375° oven for 10 to 12 minutes or till done. Immediately remove and cool on paper towels. Makes 8 cups of cookies.

Candy Canes

Hang these peppermint cookie canes on your Christmas tree for colorful ornaments. (Pictured on page 20 and on the cover.)

1 cup butter *or* margarine
1 cup sifted powdered sugar
1 egg
½ teaspoon vanilla
½ teaspoon peppermint
   extract
   Dash salt
2½ cups all-purpose flour
½ teaspoon red food coloring
   Peppermint Glaze (optional)

● In a large mixer bowl beat butter or margarine till softened. Add powdered sugar and beat till fluffy. Add egg, vanilla, peppermint extract, and salt. Beat well. Add flour and beat till well mixed. Divide dough in half. Stir food coloring into one half. Cover each half and chill about 30 minutes or till easy to handle.

● For each cookie, on a lightly floured surface shape a teaspoonful of plain dough into a 4-inch rope. Repeat with a teaspoonful of red dough. Place ropes side by side and twist together. Pinch ends to seal. Form twisted ropes into a cane. Place canes 2 inches apart on an ungreased cookie sheet.

● Bake in a 375° oven for 8 to 10 minutes or till done. Remove and cool. If desired, brush with Peppermint Glaze. Makes 48.

Peppermint Glaze: Stir together 1 cup sifted *powdered sugar,* ¼ teaspoon *peppermint extract,* and enough *water* (4 to 5 teaspoons) to make of brushing consistency.

Buried Cherry Cookies

These chocolaty cookies tied with Spritz (see recipe, page 36) for the most votes as food editors' favorites.

1 10-ounce jar (about 48)
   maraschino cherries
1½ cups all-purpose flour
½ cup unsweetened cocoa
   powder
¼ teaspoon baking soda
¼ teaspoon baking powder
¼ teaspoon salt
½ cup butter *or* margarine
1 cup sugar
1 egg
1½ teaspoons vanilla
1 6-ounce package (1 cup)
   semisweet chocolate
   pieces (*not* imitation)
½ cup *sweetened condensed*
   milk

● Drain cherries and reserve juice. Stir together flour, cocoa powder, baking soda, baking powder, and salt. In a large mixer bowl beat butter or margarine till softened. Add sugar and beat till fluffy. Add egg and vanilla and beat well. Add flour mixture and beat till well mixed.

● Shape dough into 1-inch balls. Place about 2 inches apart on an ungreased cookie sheet. Press down center of each with your thumb. Place a cherry in each center.

● For frosting, in a small saucepan combine chocolate and sweetened condensed milk. Cook and stir over low heat till chocolate is melted. Stir in *4 teaspoons* reserved cherry juice. Spoon 1 teaspoon frosting over each cherry, spreading to cover cherry. (Frosting may be thinned with additional cherry juice if necessary.) Bake in a 350° oven about 10 minutes or till done. Remove and cool. Makes about 48.

Swirled Mint Cookies

Light, crisp, and pretty. (Pictured on pages 6 and 35.)

2 cups all-purpose flour
½ teaspoon baking powder
1 cup butter *or* margarine
1 cup sugar
1 egg
1 teaspoon vanilla
½ teaspoon peppermint
    extract
10 drops red food coloring
10 drops green food coloring

● Combine flour and baking powder. In a large mixer bowl beat butter or margarine till softened. Add sugar and beat till fluffy. Add egg, vanilla, and peppermint extract and beat well. Add flour mixture and beat till well mixed. Divide into thirds. Stir red food coloring into one third, stir green food coloring into another, and leave remaining third plain. Cover each and chill about 1 hour or till easy to handle.

● Divide each color of dough into four parts. On a lightly floured surface roll each into a ½-inch-diameter rope. Place one red, one green, and one plain rope side by side. Twist together. Slice into ½-inch pieces for larger cookies or ¼-inch pieces for smaller ones. Carefully roll into balls, blending colors as little as possible. Place about 2 inches apart on an ungreased cookie sheet.

● Flatten to ¼-inch thickness with the bottom of a glass dipped in additional sugar. Repeat with remaining dough. Bake in a 375° oven till done (allow 8 to 10 minutes for larger cookies or 6 to 8 minutes for smaller ones). Remove and cool. Makes about 72 (2½-inch) or 144 (1¼-inch) cookies.

Making colored swirls
Divide the dough into thirds and tint one third red and one third green. Leave the remaining third plain. Roll each of the doughs into ½-inch-diameter ropes. Using one rope of each color, twist together to swirl the colors.

Slice the twisted ropes into ½-inch or ¼-inch pieces, depending on how big you want the cookies. Without blending the colors too much to keep them distinct, shape each slice into a ball. Place on a cookie sheet and flatten to ¼-inch thickness with the bottom of a glass that you've dipped in sugar.

Double Chocolate Dips

Dip the ends of these chocolate cookies in melted chocolate for a double dose.

2 squares (2 ounces)
   semisweet chocolate
¾ cup butter *or* margarine
⅓ cup sugar
2 tablespoons milk
1 teaspoon vanilla
2 cups all-purpose flour
5 squares (5 ounces)
   semisweet chocolate
1 tablespoon shortening
¾ cup finely chopped nuts
   (optional)

● In a heavy small saucepan heat 2 squares chocolate over low heat till melted, stirring constantly. Remove from heat and cool.

● In a large mixer bowl beat butter or margarine till softened. Add sugar and beat till fluffy. Add milk, vanilla, and cooled, melted chocolate. Beat well. Add flour and beat till well mixed.

● Using about 1 tablespoon of dough for each cookie, shape into a 2x½-inch log. Curve slightly to form a crescent shape. Place on an ungreased cookie sheet. Bake in a 325° oven about 18 minutes or till done. Remove and cool.

● Heat together 5 squares chocolate and shortening till melted. Dip two-thirds of each cookie into melted chocolate mixture. Place on waxed paper. If desired, immediately sprinkle dipped ends with nuts. Let cool till chocolate is set. Makes about 36.

Using Leftover Melted Chocolate

Often when melting chocolate for dipping or spreading on cookies, you end up with more of the luscious stuff than you need. Here are a few ideas for salvaging the leftovers, no matter how tiny an amount you have.

● Save the chocolate for other cookie recipes that require melted chocolate for dipping or spreading, such as *Florentines* on page 77 or *Cappuccino Flats* on page 84. Store the unused melted chocolate in a tightly covered storage container in the refrigerator. To use,

melt it with the additional chocolate you'll need for that recipe.

● Reuse the chocolate in the form of chunks or chips in cookie doughs such as *Chocolate Chip-Pecan Mounds* on the opposite page or *Three-in-One Cookies* on page 80. Line a cookie sheet with waxed paper and spread the remaining melted chocolate on the waxed paper. Chill in the refrigerator till firm. Then break or chop the chocolate into pieces. Cover and store the pieces in the refrigerator till ready to use.

Chocolate Chip-Pecan Mounds

Toffee-flavored bites brimming with chocolate and coated with nuts.

1 cup butter *or* margarine
1 cup packed brown sugar
1 egg yolk
1 teaspoon vanilla
2 cups all-purpose flour
1 6-ounce package (1 cup)
    semisweet chocolate
    pieces *or* miniature
    semisweet chocolate
    pieces
2 slightly beaten egg whites
2 cups finely chopped pecans

● In a large mixer bowl beat butter or margarine till softened. Add brown sugar and beat till fluffy. Add egg yolk and vanilla and beat well. Add flour and beat till well mixed. Stir in chocolate pieces. Cover and chill about 1 hour or till easy to handle.

● Shape into 1-inch balls. Roll in egg whites, then in nuts. Place on a lightly greased cookie sheet. Bake in a 350° oven about 15 minutes or till done. (Centers will still be soft.) Remove and cool. Makes about 60.

Dutch Letters

This version of Dutch Letters is more cookielike than the flaky pastry type. Though the "S" is traditional, you can shape the dough into any letter you like.

1 8-ounce can (1 cup) almond
    paste
1 egg
¼ cup sugar
1½ cups butter *or* margarine
3 cups all-purpose flour
¼ cup ice water
1 egg yolk
1 tablespoon water

● For filling, in a small mixer bowl combine almond paste, egg, and sugar and beat till smooth. Cover and chill in the refrigerator for 1½ hours or in the freezer for 30 minutes. For dough, in a large mixing bowl cut butter or margarine into flour till mixture resembles coarse crumbs. Sprinkle *1 tablespoon* ice water over part of the mixture. Gently toss with a fork and push to side of bowl. Repeat with remaining ice water till all is moistened. Form into a ball. Cover and let stand for 30 minutes.

● Divide dough into thirds. Roll each into an 8-inch square. Cut each square into four 8x2-inch strips. With moistened hands, roll about 1½ tablespoons filling into a 7½-inch rope. Repeat to make 12 ropes total. Place one rope on each strip of dough and wrap dough around filling. Seal edges and ends. Shape into "S" shapes or other letters (use family members' initials if desired). Place on an ungreased cookie sheet.

● Combine egg yolk and 1 tablespoon water and brush on letters. Bake in a 375° oven for 30 to 35 minutes or till golden. Remove and cool. To store more than one day, wrap and freeze. Makes 12.

Stuffed Stockings

Stuff colorful cookie stockings with surprises of nuts and chocolate chips.

1¾ cups all-purpose flour
½ teaspoon baking powder
¼ teaspoon salt
⅓ cup shortening
⅓ cup butter *or* margarine
⅔ cup sugar
1 egg
1 teaspoon vanilla
 Food coloring (3 colors)
½ cup semisweet chocolate pieces
½ cup chopped nuts
 Fleecy Icing

● Stir together flour, baking powder, and salt. In a large mixer bowl beat shortening and butter or margarine till butter is softened. Add sugar and beat till fluffy. Add egg and vanilla and beat well. Add flour mixture and beat till well mixed. Divide dough into thirds. Tint each third with six to eight drops of a different food coloring. Cover and chill about 1 hour or till easy to handle.

● On a lightly floured surface roll each third into a 9x6-inch rectangle. Cut each into nine 3x2-inch rectangles. Sprinkle about ½ teaspoon *each* of the chocolate pieces and nuts lengthwise down center of each rectangle. Bring long sides together, pinching to seal. Pinch ends to seal. Form into a stocking shape.

● Place seam side down on an ungreased cookie sheet. Bake in a 325° oven for 15 to 20 minutes or till done. Remove and cool. Spread with Fleecy Icing to make cuff, heel, and toe. Makes 27.

Fleecy Icing: Combine ½ cup sifted *powdered sugar,* 1 teaspoon softened *butter or margarine,* and enough *milk* (about 2 teaspoons) to make it spreadable.

Berliner Kranser

These buttery Norwegian wreaths literally melt in your mouth.

1 cup butter *or* margarine
½ cup sifted powdered sugar
1 hard-cooked egg yolk, sieved
1 raw egg yolk
1 teaspoon vanilla
2¼ cups all-purpose flour
1 slightly beaten egg white
6 to 8 sugar cubes, crushed

● In a large mixer bowl beat butter or margarine till softened. Add powdered sugar and beat till fluffy. Beat in both egg yolks and the vanilla. Stir in flour till well mixed. Cover and chill about 1 hour.

● Using about 1 tablespoon dough for each cookie, roll into 6-inch ropes. Shape each rope into a ring, overlapping about 1 inch from ends. Brush with egg white and sprinkle with crushed sugar cubes. Place on an ungreased cookie sheet. Bake in a 325° oven for 18 to 20 minutes or till done. Cool on the cookie sheet about 1 minute, then remove and cool thoroughly. Makes about 36.

Stuff and trim the stockings using these helpful hints.

1 Shaping the stockings
Sprinkle the chocolate and nuts lengthwise down the center of each rectangle of dough. Bring the two sides together over the filling and pinch the side seam and ends to keep the filling inside.

Bend the filled dough so that about one third forms the foot of the stocking. Flatten the other end slightly to look like the straight-edged top of the stocking.

2 Adding the icing
If the cookies didn't look like stockings before, they will when you add the details with icing. Cool the baked cookies before you ice. Warm cookies will melt the icing, and it will run off. Spread the icing on the top of the stocking to look like the cuff, then on the other points for the heel and the toe.

Bourbon Balls

For a milder bourbon flavor, use ¼ cup bourbon plus 1 tablespoon water.

1 6-ounce package (1 cup) semisweet chocolate pieces
¼ cup sugar
3 tablespoons light corn syrup
⅓ cup bourbon
2½ cups finely crushed vanilla wafers (about 55 wafers)
½ cup finely chopped walnuts

● In a heavy medium saucepan heat chocolate pieces over low heat till melted, stirring constantly. Remove from the heat. Stir in sugar and corn syrup. Stir in bourbon till well mixed.

● Add vanilla wafers and nuts to chocolate mixture and mix well. Let stand about 30 minutes. Shape into 1-inch balls. Roll in additional sugar. Store in a tightly covered container about one week to mellow flavor. Makes about 50.

Rum Balls: Prepare Bourbon Balls as directed above, *except* substitute *rum* for the bourbon.

Snowcapped Fudge Cookies

Store in a tightly covered container to keep them moist and chewy. (Pictured on page 30.)

4 squares (4 ounces) unsweetened chocolate
2 cups all-purpose flour
2 teaspoons baking powder
1½ cups sugar
½ cup cooking oil
2 tablespoons milk
2 teaspoons vanilla
3 eggs
2 tablespoons sugar
⅔ cup flaked coconut

● In a heavy medium saucepan heat chocolate over low heat till melted, stirring constantly. Remove from the heat and cool.

● Stir together flour and baking powder. In a large mixer bowl combine 1½ cups sugar, oil, milk, vanilla, and melted chocolate. Separate the white of *one* egg from the yolk. Place the egg white in a small mixer bowl and set aside. Add egg yolk and remaining eggs to the chocolate mixture and beat well. Add flour mixture and beat till well mixed. Cover and chill for 1 to 2 hours or till easy to handle. Clean beaters well.

● Shape dough into 1-inch balls. Place 2 inches apart on an ungreased cookie sheet. Flatten slightly with your fingers. Beat reserved egg white with electric mixer on medium speed till soft peaks form. Gradually add 2 tablespoons sugar, beating on high speed till stiff peaks form. Fold in coconut. Top each flattened ball of dough with ½ teaspoon of the coconut mixture.

● Bake in a 375° oven for 10 to 12 minutes or till cookies are done and tops are light brown. Remove and cool. Makes 48.

Butter Pecan Nuggets

Toast the pecan halves to bring out their flavor before tucking one inside each ball of dough. (Pictured on page 30.)

¾ cup pecan halves (about 48)
1 cup butter *or* margarine
⅔ cup packed brown sugar
1 teaspoon vanilla
2½ cups all-purpose flour
1 cup sifted powdered sugar
½ teaspoon vanilla
4 to 5 teaspoons milk
 Colored sugar (optional)

● Spread pecans in a single layer on a cookie sheet. Toast in a 325° oven about 12 minutes or till golden. Remove and cool.

● In a medium saucepan combine butter or margarine and brown sugar. Heat and stir till butter is melted. Remove from the heat. Stir in 1 teaspoon vanilla. Cool.

● Stir in flour till well mixed. Shape into ¾-inch balls. Press a toasted pecan half into each ball and enclose nut in dough to form an oval. Place on an ungreased cookie sheet. Bake in the 325° oven for 18 to 20 minutes or till done. Remove and cool.

● Stir together the powdered sugar, ½ teaspoon vanilla, and enough milk to make of pouring consistency. Drizzle over cookies. If desired, sprinkle with colored sugar. Makes about 48.

Maple Yule Logs

Though tradition says that a Yule log be oak, pine, or ash, maple is a tastier choice for these cookies. (Pictured on page 30.)

¾ cup butter *or* margarine
¾ cup packed brown sugar
1 egg
1½ teaspoons maple flavoring
½ teaspoon salt
2 cups all-purpose flour
¼ cup butter *or* margarine
3 to 3¼ cups sifted powdered sugar
3 tablespoons milk
1 teaspoon maple flavoring

● In a large mixer bowl beat ¾ cup butter or margarine till softened. Add brown sugar and beat till fluffy. Add egg, 1½ teaspoons maple flavoring, and salt and beat well. Add flour and beat till well mixed. Cover and chill about 1 hour or till easy to handle.

● Divide dough into eight parts. On a lightly floured surface roll each eighth into a rope ½ inch in diameter. Cut into logs about 3 inches long. Place on an ungreased cookie sheet. Bake in a 375° oven for 8 to 10 minutes or till done. Remove and cool.

● For frosting, in a small mixer bowl beat ¼ cup butter or margarine till light and fluffy. Gradually add about *half* of the powdered sugar, beating well. Beat in milk and 1 teaspoon maple flavoring. Gradually beat in enough of the remaining powdered sugar to make frosting spreadable. Frost tops and sides of cookies, swirling frosting to resemble bark. Makes 48.

Kringla

Snowmen

Snowcapped Fudge
Cookies
(see recipe, page 28)

Butter Pecan Nuggets
(see recipe, page 29)

Maple Yule Logs
(see recipe, page 29)

Snowmen

Top off each snowman with a handmade gumdrop hat. (Also pictured on page 6.)

1 cup butter *or* margarine
½ cup sugar
1 teaspoon vanilla
2¼ cups all-purpose flour
   Miniature semisweet
     chocolate pieces
   Powdered Sugar Icing
   Thin ribbon *or* shoestring
     licorice
   Large gumdrops
   Powdered sugar
   Food coloring (optional)

● In a large mixer bowl beat butter or margarine till softened. Add sugar and beat till fluffy. Beat in vanilla. Add flour and beat till well mixed. For each snowman, shape dough into three balls: one 1-inch ball, one ¾-inch ball, and one ½-inch ball.

● Place balls on an ungreased cookie sheet in decreasing sizes with sides touching. Press together slightly. Insert two chocolate pieces in smallest ball for eyes, then one in middle ball and two in largest ball for buttons. Bake in a 325° oven for 18 to 20 minutes or till done. Carefully remove and cool.

● Prepare Powdered Sugar Icing. Tie a 6-inch piece of ribbon or licorice around the neck of each snowman. For each hat, sprinkle additional sugar on a cutting board. Place one gumdrop on sugared board and sprinkle with more sugar. With a rolling pin, roll gumdrop into an oval about ⅛ inch thick. Curve to form a cone and press together to seal. If desired, bend up edge for brim. Attach to head with the icing. Lightly sprinkle snowmen with powdered sugar. If broom is desired, tint remaining icing with food coloring and pipe onto cookies. Makes about 24.

Powdered Sugar Icing: Combine ¾ cup sifted *powdered sugar* and enough *milk* (about 1 tablespoon) to make it spreadable.

Kringla

A beloved Norwegian favorite. The soft dough bakes into a cakelike cookie.

3 cups all-purpose flour
2½ teaspoons baking powder
1 teaspoon baking soda
½ teaspoon salt
¼ teaspoon ground nutmeg *or*
   cardamom (optional)
½ cup butter *or* margarine
1 cup sugar
1 egg
1 teaspoon vanilla
¾ cup buttermilk

● Stir together flour, baking powder, baking soda, salt, and nutmeg or cardamom. In a large mixer bowl beat butter or margarine till softened. Add sugar and beat till fluffy. Add egg and vanilla and beat well. Add flour mixture and buttermilk alternately, beating till well mixed. Cover and chill about 4 hours or overnight.

● Divide dough in half. On a floured surface roll each half into a 10x5-inch rectangle. With a sharp knife, cut each into twenty 5x½-inch strips. Roll each into a 10-inch rope. Shape into a loop, crossing 1½ inches from ends. Twist rope at crossing point. Lift loop over to ends and seal, forming a pretzel shape.

● Place on an ungreased cookie sheet. Bake in a 425° oven about 5 minutes or till done (tops will be pale). Remove and cool. Makes 40.

Cardamom Print Wafers

The more you flatten them, the crisper the cookies and the better the cookie stamp imprint shows up. (Pictured on page 35.)

1¾ cups all-purpose flour
½ teaspoon ground cardamom
½ teaspoon ground cinnamon
¼ teaspoon salt
½ cup butter *or* margarine
¾ cup packed brown sugar
1 egg
½ teaspoon vanilla

● Stir together flour, cardamom, cinnamon, and salt. In a small mixer bowl beat butter or margarine till softened. Add brown sugar and beat till fluffy. Add egg and vanilla and beat well. Stir in flour mixture till well mixed. Cover and chill about 2 hours or till easy to handle.

● Shape into ¾-inch balls. Place 2 inches apart on a greased cookie sheet. Flatten firmly with a floured cookie stamp or the floured bottom of a glass that has a design in it. Bake in a 350° oven about 8 minutes or till done. Remove and cool. Makes about 96.

Hazelnut Snaps

Elegant, lacy, and almost like candy. (Pictured on page 15.)

½ cup packed brown sugar
½ cup butter *or* margarine
⅓ cup corn syrup
1 cup ground hazelnuts
   (filberts)
¾ cup all-purpose flour
2 tablespoons hazelnut
   liqueur *or* brandy

● In a small saucepan combine brown sugar, butter, and corn syrup. Cook and stir over medium heat till well blended. Remove from the heat. Stir in hazelnuts, flour, and liqueur.

● Drop from a teaspoon about 5 inches apart onto a greased foil-lined cookie sheet. (Bake only four or five at a time.) Bake in a 350° oven for 9 to 11 minutes or till done.

● Let stand for 1 minute. Remove from cookie sheet, one at a time, and shape as desired (pull up three sides to center to form a triangle or roll around the greased handle of a wooden spoon). Cool. Makes about 48.

Softening Cookies for Shaping

Cookies such as *Hazelnut Snaps* and *Cinnamon Curls* need to be shaped immediately after baking, while they are still flexible. As the cookies cool, they become stiff and difficult to shape. If the baked cookies harden before you can shape them, simply return them to the hot oven about 1 minute or till softened.

Cinnamon Curls

Bake only two cookies at once to allow yourself time to roll up the cookies before they harden.

2 egg whites
½ cup sugar
½ cup all-purpose flour
1 teaspoon ground cinnamon
¼ cup butter *or* margarine,
    melted and cooled

● In a small mixer bowl beat egg whites till soft peaks form. Gradually add sugar, beating till stiff peaks form. Combine flour and cinnamon and stir into egg whites. Stir in cooled, melted butter or margarine till well mixed.

● Generously grease two 4-inch circles on a cookie sheet. Drop a small mound of batter (two level measuring teaspoonfuls) onto each greased spot. Spread with the back of a spoon into 3-inch circles.

● Bake in a 350° oven for 6 to 8 minutes or till done. Immediately loosen and roll around the greased handle of a wooden spoon. Slide off cookie and cool. Repeat with remaining batter, using a clean, greased circle on cookie sheet for each. Makes 24 to 30.

Note: You can bake up to three two-cookie batches before washing the cookie sheet. Grease two circles on opposite sides of the cookie sheet for the first batch. For the second and third batches, grease areas on the cookie sheet that have not been used.

Rolling up the cookies

As soon as the cookies are golden on the edges, loosen them from the cookie sheet with a pancake turner. Working quickly to prevent hardening, roll the first cookie around the handle of a greased wooden spoon. Work with the bowl of the spoon over the edge of the counter to make rolling smoother. Slip off the cookie onto a cooling rack and repeat with the second one.

If the cookies harden before you can shape them, put them back in the oven about 1 minute to rewarm and soften.

Pizzelles

Bake these Italian wafer cookies in a pizzelle (piz-ZEL-ee) iron. (Also pictured on page 7.)

  2   cups all-purpose flour
  1   tablespoon baking powder
1½   teaspoons ground nutmeg
  ½   teaspoon ground cardamom
  3   eggs
  ¾   cup sugar
  ⅓   cup butter *or* margarine,
        melted and cooled
  2   teaspoons vanilla

● Stir together flour, baking powder, nutmeg, and cardamom. In a small mixer bowl beat eggs with an electric mixer on high speed about 4 minutes or till thick and lemon colored. With mixer on medium speed, gradually beat in sugar. Beat in cooled, melted butter or margarine and vanilla. Add flour mixture and beat on low speed till combined.

● Heat pizzelle iron on range-top over medium heat (or heat an electric pizzelle iron according to manufacturer's directions) till a drop of water sizzles on the grid. Reduce heat to medium-low. Place a slightly rounded tablespoon of batter in the center of the round grid. Squeeze lid to close. Bake for 30 to 60 seconds or till golden, turning iron once. (Or, use an electric pizzelle iron according to manufacturer's directions.) Turn wafer out onto a paper towel to cool. Repeat with remaining batter. Makes 18.

Sandbakelser

If you don't have the tiny molds to make these rich Swedish "sand tarts," shape the dough into balls and flatten for an exceptional butter cookie.

  ½   cup butter *or* margarine
  ½   cup sugar
  1   egg yolk
  ¼   teaspoon almond extract
1⅓   cups all-purpose flour

● If necessary, season 2½-inch sandbakelser molds.* In a small mixer bowl beat butter or margarine till softened. Add sugar and beat till fluffy. Add egg yolk and extract and beat well. Add flour and beat till well mixed.

● Place about 2 teaspoons of dough in the center of a seasoned 2½-inch sandbakelser mold. Press dough evenly and very thinly over bottom and up sides. Repeat with remaining dough. Place molds on a cookie sheet.

● Or, form dough into 1-inch balls. Place on an ungreased cookie sheet. Flatten to ¼-inch thickness with the bottom of a glass dipped in additional sugar. If desired, make designs in the dough with the tip of a spoon.

● Bake in a 375° oven for 8 to 10 minutes or till edges are lightly browned. For molded cookies, cool *in molds*. To remove, invert molds and tap lightly. Loosen with a toothpick, if necessary. For flattened cookies, remove and cool. Makes 24 to 30.

*To season sandbakelser molds, grease inside of molds with shortening. Heat in a 300° oven for 30 minutes. Cool. Wipe out excess shortening. After use, rinse with water and wipe out with paper towels. No further seasoning is needed.

Spritz
(see recipe, page 36)

Pizzelles

Cardamom Print Wafers
(see recipe, page 32)

Swirled Mint Cookies
(see recipe, page 23)

Sandbakelser

Spritz

Turn out cookies shaped like trees, wreaths, and more with a manual or electric cookie press. (Pictured on pages 7 and 35.)

3½ cups all-purpose flour
1 teaspoon baking powder
1½ cups butter *or* margarine
1 cup sugar
1 egg
1 teaspoon vanilla
½ teaspoon almond extract
Food coloring (optional)
Colored sugars *or* decorative candies (optional)

● Stir together flour and baking powder. In a large mixer bowl beat butter or margarine till softened. Add sugar and beat till fluffy. Add egg, vanilla, and almond extract and beat well. Gradually add flour mixture and beat till well mixed. To ensure easy passage through the cookie press, do not chill dough.

● If desired, tint dough with food coloring. Force dough through a cookie press onto an ungreased cookie sheet. Decorate with colored sugars or candies, if desired. Bake in a 400° oven for 7 to 8 minutes or till done. Remove and cool. Makes about 60.

Krumkake

Bake these in a Scandinavian krumkake (KROOM-kah-kah) iron over a gas or electric burner.

3 eggs
½ cup sugar
½ cup butter *or* margarine, melted and cooled
1 teaspoon vanilla
½ cup all-purpose flour

● In a small mixing bowl beat eggs and sugar with a rotary beater or wire whisk till well mixed. Stir in cooled, melted butter or margarine and vanilla. Beat in flour till smooth.

● Heat krumkake iron on range-top over medium-high heat. For a 6-inch iron, drop about ½ tablespoon batter onto the hot, ungreased iron. Close gently but firmly. Bake over medium-high heat for 15 to 20 seconds or till light golden brown. Turn iron over and bake 15 to 20 seconds more. Loosen with a knife and remove with a pancake turner. Immediately shape around a wooden or metal roller or roll up with your hands. Reheat iron and repeat with remaining batter. Makes about 48.

CUTOUT COOKIES

Get out
the rolling pin and get
ready to have some fun.
Think of the assortment of
cookies you can make just
by using different cookie
cutters! Let the shapes
inspire you to decorate them
for even more variety.
Even if you don't have a
cookie cutter in your
kitchen, you're still in the
game. For example, Apricot
Twists and Chocolate-
Coconut Pinwheels are cut
out with a knife, then
formed into eye-catching
shapes.

Cutout Cookie Hints

Chilling the Dough

To firm up the dough so it won't stick to the rolling pin or surface, chill it in the refrigerator. Divide the dough into halves or thirds for faster chilling. Gather each part into a flat loaf (instead of a ball, which would take longer to chill) and wrap in clear plastic wrap. Roll and cut out only one part of the dough at a time, keeping the remainder chilled so it stays firm.

To speed the chilling even more, put the dough in the freezer. As a general rule, chill in the freezer about 20 minutes for every hour needed in the refrigerator. If the dough becomes too stiff to roll out, let it stand at room temperature until it softens a bit.

Rolling Out The Dough

Unless otherwise stated, roll dough on a lightly floured surface such as a pastry cloth or countertop. Using a floured rolling pin, work from the center to edges.

Roll the dough as thick as the recipe specifies. Use a ruler to be sure that all of the dough is the same thickness for even baking.

Reroll scraps left from the cutouts to cut more cookies. Though rerolling can toughen dough, rerolling on a surface dusted with a mixture of equal parts flour and powdered sugar will toughen it less than rerolling on flour alone.

Cutting Out and Decorating the Cookies

Cut the dough into shapes, using cookie cutters dusted with flour to prevent sticking. Or cut out shapes with a sharp knife, using a cardboard pattern if you like. Make cutouts as close together as possible. Lift them to the cookie sheet with a pancake turner.

Sprinkle with colored sugar, nuts, or decorative candies *before* baking so the decorations will stick. Frost cookies after baking and cooling.

When Are They Done?

Bake cutout cookies till they are very lightly browned around the edges. To keep the cookies from sticking to one another, do not stack or store them until they are thoroughly cooled.

Apricot Twists

A twist from typical cookies because they're flaky like pastry. (Pictured on page 41.)

2 cups all-purpose flour
⅓ cup sugar
½ teaspoon salt
½ teaspoon ground mace
¼ teaspoon baking powder
¾ cup butter *or* margarine
5 to 7 tablespoons ice water
¼ teaspoon lemon extract
¼ cup apricot *or* pineapple
  preserves
Milk

● Stir together flour, sugar, salt, mace, and baking powder. Cut in butter or margarine till mixture resembles coarse crumbs. Combine *1 tablespoon* of the ice water and the lemon extract and sprinkle over part of the mixture. Gently toss with a fork and push to side of bowl. Repeat with remaining ice water, a tablespoon at a time, till all is moistened. Form into a ball. Cover and chill about 30 minutes or till easy to handle.

● Divide dough into quarters. Roll two of the quarters into 12x4-inch rectangles and spread with preserves. Roll remaining two quarters into 12x4-inch rectangles and carefully place over those spread with preserves. Trim edges.

● Cut each rectangle into twelve 4x1-inch strips. Twist each strip twice. Place on an ungreased cookie sheet. Bake in a 375° oven for 15 minutes. Remove and brush with milk, then sprinkle with additional sugar. Return to oven and bake 5 to 8 minutes more or till done. Remove and cool. Makes 24.

Sour Cream Spice Knots

Bake these lightly spiced cookies just till the edges start to brown. They should be crisp on the edges and soft at the twisted center. (Pictured on page 41.)

2¾ cups all-purpose flour
½ teaspoon baking soda
¼ teaspoon salt
¼ teaspoon ground nutmeg
2 tablespoons sugar
½ teaspoon ground cinnamon
½ cup butter *or* margarine
1 cup sugar
1 egg
½ teaspoon vanilla
½ cup dairy sour cream

● Combine flour, baking soda, salt, and nutmeg. In a small bowl combine 2 tablespoons sugar and the cinnamon and set aside.

● In a large mixer bowl beat butter or margarine till softened. Add 1 cup sugar and beat till fluffy. Add egg and vanilla and beat well. Add flour mixture and sour cream alternately, beating till well mixed. Divide dough in half. Cover and chill at least 2 hours or till easy to handle.

● Roll dough ⅛ inch thick. Cut into rings with a 2½-inch doughnut cutter. Twist rings once to form figure eights. Place 2 inches apart on an ungreased cookie sheet. Sprinkle with cinnamon-sugar mixture. Bake in a 350° oven for 6 to 8 minutes or till done. Remove and cool. Makes about 60.

Fruit and Spice Rounds

Another way to make these moist, chewy cookies is to shape the dough into 1¼-inch balls and flatten with a sugared glass.

2 cups all-purpose flour
1 teaspoon baking soda
1 teaspoon salt
1 teaspoon ground cinnamon
¾ teaspoon ground cloves
½ teaspoon ground nutmeg
1 cup raisins
1 cup dried figs
1 cup pitted whole dates
½ cup broken walnuts
1 cup butter *or* margarine
1½ cups sugar
3 eggs
    Vanilla Icing

● Stir together flour, baking soda, salt, cinnamon, cloves, and nutmeg. In a food processor bowl or with the fine blade of a food grinder, process or grind raisins, figs, dates, and walnuts.

● In a large mixer bowl beat butter or margarine till softened. Add sugar and beat till fluffy. Add eggs and beat well. Add flour mixture and beat till well mixed. Stir in ground fruit mixture. Divide dough in half. Cover and chill several hours or overnight.

● On a well-floured surface roll dough ¼ inch thick. Cut into rounds with a 2½-inch cookie cutter. Place on a greased cookie sheet. Bake in a 375° oven for 10 to 12 minutes or till done. Cool on cookie sheet for 2 to 3 minutes, then remove and cool thoroughly. Drizzle with Vanilla Icing. Makes about 60.

Vanilla Icing: In a small mixing bowl combine 1½ cups sifted *powdered sugar,* 1 tablespoon softened *butter or margarine,* ½ teaspoon *vanilla,* and enough *milk* (4 to 5 teaspoons) to make icing of drizzling consistency.

Pastel Cream Wafers

Make the wafers with butter, not margarine, for a firm, manageable, and rich-tasting pastry.

6 tablespoons cold butter
1 cup all-purpose flour
3 to 4 tablespoons light cream
    Sugar
1 cup sifted powdered sugar
1 tablespoon softened butter
½ teaspoon vanilla
1 drop food coloring
    About 1 tablespoon light
      cream

● In a medium mixing bowl cut 6 tablespoons butter into flour till pieces are the size of small peas. Sprinkle *1 tablespoon* of the cream over part of mixture. Gently toss with a fork and push to side of bowl. Repeat till all is moistened. Form into a ball.

● Roll dough slightly less than ⅛ inch thick. Cut into rounds with a 1½-inch cookie cutter. Dip one side of each round of dough in sugar. Place, sugar side up, on an ungreased cookie sheet. With a fork, prick each in four parallel rows. Bake in a 375° oven for 8 to 10 minutes or till edges just begin to brown. Remove and cool.

● For filling, in a small bowl stir together powdered sugar, 1 tablespoon softened butter, vanilla, food coloring, and enough of the 1 tablespoon cream to make it spreadable. Spread ½ teaspoon filling on the flat side of *half* of the cookies. Top with the remaining cookies, flat side down. Makes 24.

Fruit and Spice Rounds

Apricot Twists
(see recipe, page 39)

Pastel Cream Wafers

Chocolate-Coconut
Pinwheels
(see recipe, page 44)

Sour Cream Spice Knots
(see recipe, page 39)

Rolled Sugar Cookies

Decorate these basic cutouts any way you like. To turn them into ornaments for your tree, see the instructions on page 8. (Pictured on pages 6 and 7 and on the cover.)

2 cups all-purpose flour
1½ teaspoons baking powder
¼ teaspoon salt
6 tablespoons butter *or* margarine
⅓ cup shortening
¾ cup sugar
1 egg
1 tablespoon milk
1 teaspoon vanilla
Creamy Decorative Icing (optional)
Decorative candies (optional)

● Stir together flour, baking powder, and salt. In a large mixer bowl beat butter and shortening till butter is softened. Add sugar and beat till fluffy. Add egg, milk, and vanilla and beat well. Add flour mixture and beat till well mixed. Divide dough in half. Cover and chill at least 3 hours or till easy to handle.

● Roll dough ⅛ inch thick. Cut with cookie cutters. Place on an ungreased cookie sheet. Bake in a 375° oven for 7 to 8 minutes or till done. Remove and cool. If desired, pipe on Creamy Decorative Icing with a decorating bag and decorate with candies. Makes 36 to 48.

Candy Window Sugar Cookies: Prepare the dough for Rolled Sugar Cookies as above. Roll out and cut into desired shapes. Place on a foil-lined cookie sheet. Cut out small shapes in the cookie centers. Finely crush 3 ounces *clear hard candy* and spoon enough into each center to fill hole. Bake as directed till done. Peel off foil and cool.

Creamy Decorative Icing: In a small mixer bowl beat 1 *egg white,* 2 teaspoons *lemon juice,* and enough sifted *powdered sugar* (1½ to 2 cups) to make icing of piping consistency. If desired, stir in several drops *food coloring.*

Turn plain cookies into spectacular ones using these decorating ideas.

1 Making candy windows
Arrange the cutouts on a cookie sheet lined with foil so the candy won't stick to the cookie sheet. Cut out one or more small shapes in the middle of each cutout using tiny hors d'oeuvre cutters, a thimble, or a sharp knife.

Crush hard candy into fine pieces by placing it in a plastic bag and pounding it with a rolling pin, the flat edge of a meat mallet, or a hammer. Spoon enough of the candy into the cutout centers to fill the hole to the level of the dough. If you use more than one color per hole, mix the colors as little as possible. As the cookies bake, the candy will melt into smooth "windowpanes."

2 Decorating with icing
After the cookies are baked and cooled, give them character with colorful creamy icing.

Fill a decorating bag no more than half full of icing. Pipe outlines on the edges of the cookies, then fill in if you like. Use a writing tip, star tip, leaf tip, or any other tip with a small opening. If you don't use all of the icing, store it in a tightly covered container in the refrigerator for several weeks.

Chocolate-Coconut Pinwheels

Cream cheese-coconut mounds hide inside these fun-shaped cookies. (Pictured on page 41.)

1¾ cups all-purpose flour
⅓ cup unsweetened cocoa powder
1½ teaspoons baking powder
¼ teaspoon salt
⅓ cup shortening
⅓ cup butter *or* margarine
¾ cup sugar
1 egg
1 tablespoon milk
1 teaspoon vanilla
1 3-ounce package cream cheese, softened
⅓ cup sugar
1 teaspoon vanilla
1 cup flaked coconut
¼ cup finely chopped walnuts *or* pecans

● Stir together flour, cocoa powder, baking powder, and salt. In a large mixer bowl beat shortening and butter till butter is softened. Add ¾ cup sugar and beat till fluffy. Add egg, milk, and 1 teaspoon vanilla and beat well. Add flour mixture and beat till well mixed. Divide dough in half. Cover and chill for 2 to 3 hours or till easy to handle.

● Meanwhile, in a small mixing bowl stir together softened cream cheese, ⅓ cup sugar, and 1 teaspoon vanilla till smooth. Stir in coconut.

● Roll each half of the dough into a 10-inch square. With a pastry wheel or sharp knife, cut each square into sixteen 2½-inch squares. Place ½ inch apart on an ungreased cookie sheet. With a knife, cut 1-inch slits from each corner to center. Drop a level teaspoon of the coconut mixture in each center. Fold every other tip to center to form a pinwheel. Sprinkle chopped nuts in center and press firmly to seal.

● Bake in a 350° oven for 8 to 10 minutes or till edges are firm and cookies are slightly puffed. Cool on cookie sheet for 1 minute, then remove and cool thoroughly. Makes 32.

Old-Fashioned Sugar Cookies

One of our editors fondly remembers her grandmother making these soft, fat sugar cookies. Her favorite size, then and now, is the great big one. (Pictured on page 6.)

4½ cups all-purpose flour
2 teaspoons baking powder
1 teaspoon baking soda
½ teaspoon salt
½ teaspoon ground nutmeg
1¼ cups shortening
2 cups sugar
2 eggs
1 teaspoon vanilla
½ teaspoon lemon extract
1 cup buttermilk *or* sour milk*

● Stir together flour, baking powder, baking soda, salt, and nutmeg. In a large mixer bowl beat shortening for 30 seconds. Add sugar and beat till fluffy. Add eggs, vanilla, and lemon extract and beat well. Add flour mixture and buttermilk alternately to shortening mixture, beating till well mixed. Divide in half. Cover and chill at least 3 hours or till easy to handle.

● For large cookies, roll dough ½ inch thick. Cut into rounds with a 3-inch cookie cutter. For small cookies, roll dough ⅜ inch thick and cut into rounds with a 2-inch cutter. Place 2½ inches apart on an ungreased cookie sheet. Sprinkle with additional sugar. Bake in a 375° oven for 10 to 12 minutes or till done. Remove and cool. Makes 24 large or 48 small cookies.

*To make sour milk, combine 1 tablespoon *lemon juice or vinegar* and enough *milk* to make 1 cup. Let stand for 5 minutes.

Scottish Shortbread

Shortbread is one of those pleasures of life that's simple, yet outstanding.

1¼ cups all-purpose flour
3 tablespoons sugar
½ cup butter *or* margarine

● In a medium mixing bowl combine the flour and sugar. Cut in butter or margarine till mixture resembles fine crumbs. Form the mixture into a ball and knead till smooth.

● For wedges, on an ungreased cookie sheet pat the dough into an 8-inch circle. Using your fingers, press to make a scalloped edge. With a fork, prick dough deeply to make 16 pie-shape wedges. Bake in a 300° oven for 40 to 50 minutes or till edges are very lightly browned and center is set. Cut along perforations while warm.

● For strips or rounds, on a lightly floured surface pat dough ½ inch thick. Cut into 24 (2x1-inch) strips with a knife or into 24 rounds with a 1½-inch cookie cutter. Place on an ungreased cookie sheet. Bake in a 300° oven about 30 minutes or till bottoms are lightly browned.

● Makes 16 wedges or 24 strips or rounds.

Spiced Shortbread: Prepare Scottish Shortbread as above, *except* substitute *brown sugar* for the sugar and stir ½ teaspoon ground *cinnamon,* ¼ teaspoon ground *ginger,* and ⅛ teaspoon ground *cloves* into the flour mixture.

Lemon-Poppy Seed Shortbread: Prepare Scottish Shortbread as above, *except* stir 1 tablespoon *poppy seed* into flour mixture and add 1 teaspoon finely shredded *lemon peel* with the butter.

Butter Pecan Shortbread: Prepare Scottish Shortbread as above, *except* substitute *brown sugar* for the sugar and stir 2 tablespoons finely chopped *pecans* into the flour mixture. After cutting in butter, sprinkle mixture with ½ teaspoon *vanilla* and knead till smooth.

Oatmeal Shortbread: Prepare Scottish Shortbread as above, *except* reduce flour to 1 cup and stir ⅓ cup quick-cooking *rolled oats* into the flour mixture.

Gingerbread Cutouts

Simple or fancy, your decorations give them their personality.

5 cups all-purpose flour
2 teaspoons ground ginger
1½ teaspoons baking soda
1 teaspoon ground cinnamon
1 teaspoon ground cloves
½ teaspoon salt
1 cup shortening
1 cup sugar
1 egg
1 cup molasses
2 tablespoons vinegar
   Creamy Decorative Icing
     (see recipe, page 42)
     and decorative candies
     (optional)

● Stir together flour, ginger, baking soda, cinnamon, cloves, and salt. In a large mixer bowl beat shortening for 30 seconds. Add sugar and beat till fluffy. Add egg, molasses, and vinegar and beat well. Beat in flour mixture, stirring in last part with a spoon till well mixed. Divide dough into thirds. Cover and chill about 3 hours or till easy to handle.

● Roll dough ⅛ inch thick. Cut with cookie cutters. Place on a greased cookie sheet. Add additional dough for hair, if desired. Bake in a 375° oven for 5 to 6 minutes or till done. Cool on cookie sheet for 1 minute, then remove and cool thoroughly. If desired, decorate with Creamy Decorative Icing and candies. Makes about 66 (6-inch) or 96 (3-inch) cookies.

Making gingerbread hair with a garlic press
Before baking gingerbread people and animals, give them hair made from the same dough.

   Place a small amount of the dough in the cavity of a garlic press. Squeeze together the handles, forcing the dough through the holes of the press. Use a knife to break off the strands and apply to the gingerbread cutouts.

Sour Cream Cutout Sandies

Instead of cutouts, you can shape the dough into 1-inch balls and bake about 10 minutes.

½ cup broken pecans
2¼ cups all-purpose flour
1½ teaspoons baking powder
½ cup butter *or* margarine
⅓ cup shortening
¾ cup sugar
1 egg
⅓ cup dairy sour cream
1 teaspoon vanilla
    Lemon Glaze
    Chopped pecans *or*
       pistachios

● Grind the ½ cup pecans with a food grinder, food processor, or blender. Combine ground pecans, flour, and baking powder. In a large mixer bowl beat butter and shortening till butter is softened. Add sugar and beat till fluffy. Add egg, sour cream, and vanilla and beat well. Add flour mixture and beat till well mixed. Divide dough in half. Cover and chill at least 3 hours or till easy to handle.

● Roll dough ⅛ inch thick. Cut with cookie cutters. Place on an ungreased cookie sheet. Bake in a 375° oven for 7 to 8 minutes or till done. Remove and cool. Spread cookies with Lemon Glaze. Sprinkle with chopped nuts. Makes about 80.

Lemon Glaze: In a small mixer bowl beat 1 *egg white* till frothy. Beat in 1½ cups sifted *powdered sugar,* and 1 tablespoon *lemon juice.* If desired, stir in a few drops *food coloring.*

Cream Cheese Cutouts

It's the cream cheese that makes them extra rich and flavorful.

1 cup butter *or* margarine
1 8-ounce package cream
       cheese
3½ cups all-purpose flour
1 teaspoon baking powder
1½ cups sugar
1 egg
1 teaspoon vanilla
½ teaspoon almond extract
    Almond Frosting

● In a large mixer bowl combine butter and cream cheese. Let stand at room temperature about 30 minutes or till softened. Stir together flour and baking powder.

● Beat together softened butter and cream cheese. Add sugar and beat till fluffy. Add egg, vanilla, and almond extract and beat well. Add flour mixture and beat till well mixed. Divide in half. Cover and chill about 1½ hours or till easy to handle.

● Roll dough ⅛ inch thick. Cut with cookie cutters. Place on an ungreased cookie sheet. Bake in a 375° oven for 8 to 10 minutes or till done. Remove and cool. Pipe or spread Almond Frosting onto cookies. Makes about 90.

Almond Frosting: In a small mixer bowl beat 2 cups sifted *powdered sugar,* 2 tablespoons softened *butter or margarine,* and ¼ teaspoon *almond extract.* Beat in enough *milk* (4 to 5 teaspoons) till of piping consistency. (For spreadable icing, add more milk.) Stir in a few drops *food coloring,* if desired.

Tiny Gingerbread Town

5 cups all-purpose flour
2 teaspoons ground ginger
1 teaspoon baking soda
1 teaspoon ground cinnamon
½ teaspoon salt
1 cup butter *or* margarine
1 cup sugar
1 cup molasses
  Snow Frosting
  Green food coloring
  Assorted candies
  Mixed whole nuts
  Powdered sugar

● Make patterns by tracing the figures on page 51 onto cardboard and cutting them out. Mix flour, ginger, baking soda, cinnamon, and salt. In a large mixer bowl beat butter till softened. Add sugar and beat till fluffy. Add molasses and beat well. Gradually beat in flour mixture, working in last part by hand.

● Divide into thirds. Roll each third ¼ inch thick directly onto an ungreased cookie sheet,* placing waxed paper over dough to prevent sticking to the rolling pin. Cut around patterns as shown on page 50. Lift off scraps and reserve. Cut *half* of the tree pieces and *one* of the steeple pieces in half from top to bottom. Give roofs and walls designs by scoring with a knife or pressing with tip of a spoon or one side of a tiny hors d'oeuvres cutter. Reroll scraps to cut number of pieces shown on page 51.

● Bake in a 375° oven for 9 to 11 minutes or till done. While cookies are still hot on cookie sheet, trim straight edges of trees, steeple, and building pieces to straighten. Remove and cool.

● Assemble trees as shown on page 50. Decorate with some of the Snow Frosting tinted with green food coloring and attach candies. Assemble buildings with Snow Frosting as shown on page 50. Let dry and decorate with frosting and candies. For church (also pictured on the cover), attach two steeple halves to whole steeple piece at right angles with frosting. Attach a small candy to steeple top. Secure steeple to roof with frosting.

● Arrange buildings and trees on a large foil-covered piece of cardboard. For pond, cut a piece of nonabsorbent colored paper into desired shape and attach to foil. With a star tip, pipe frosting around edge. (Or, pipe frosting directly onto foil for pond outline.) For fence, use a writing tip to pipe a ¾-inch-wide strip of frosting on foil, then press in nuts. Repeat layers till fence is desired height, ending with frosting. Sift powdered sugar over town for snow. Arrange candies in front of buildings for walks. Makes 3 buildings and 8 trees.

Snow Frosting: In a large mixer bowl beat 1½ cups *shortening* and 1½ teaspoons *vanilla* for 30 seconds. Gradually beat in 3½ cups sifted *powdered sugar*. Add 3 tablespoons *milk*. Gradually beat in 3½ cups more sifted *powdered sugar* and enough *milk* (3 to 4 tablespoons) to make frosting of piping consistency.

*If making a stained-glass window in church front, cover the cookie sheet with foil before rolling out dough. Cut a hole in the dough with a tiny hors d'oeuvres cutter or knife and fill hole with crushed *clear hard candies.* Bake as directed.

Tiny Gingerbread Town

Building the Tiny Gingerbread Town

1 Cutting out the dough
Roll dough directly onto a cookie sheet. (Do not flour the cookie sheet.) Place a damp towel under the cookie sheet to prevent sliding as you roll.

Place the patterns ½ inch apart on dough to allow for spreading during baking. Cut around patterns with a sharp knife, fitting as many pieces on a cookie sheet as you can.

2 Assembling the trees
For each tree, pipe or spread frosting onto the straight edge of two tree halves. Attach to a whole tree piece so the halves are at right angles to the whole. Let dry before decorating.

Tint some frosting with green food coloring and pipe onto trees with a star tip. Attach candies with more frosting.

3 Assembling the buildings
Pipe frosting along the bottom edge of the side and end pieces of each building. Place the pieces, frosting side down, on the round base. With a writing tip, join the four walls by piping frosting along the corner edges where the walls meet. Let dry before adding the roof.

When you're ready to roof, pipe frosting along the top edges of all the standing walls. Attach one roof piece, then the other.

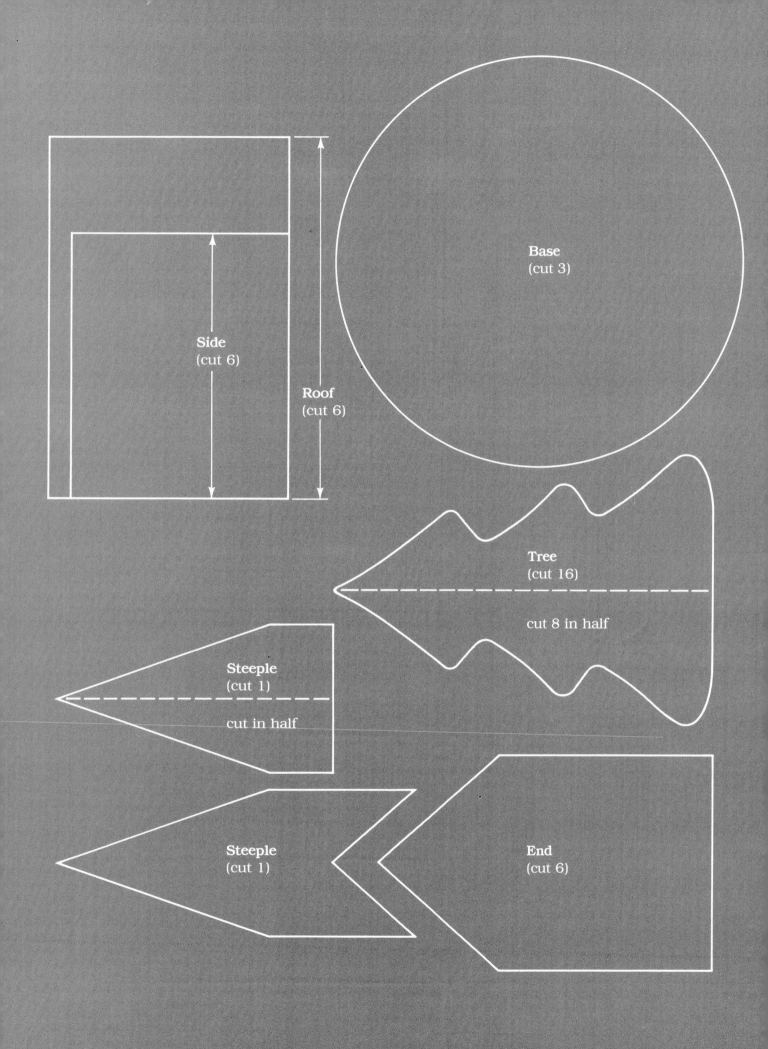

Springerle

Age these German picture cookies three days to soften them and mellow the anise flavor.

3½ cups all-purpose flour
 1 teaspoon baking soda
 4 eggs
 1 pound powdered sugar,
    sifted (about 4¾ cups)
20 drops oil of anise
    (about ¼ teaspoon)
    Crushed aniseed

● Combine flour and baking soda. In a large mixer bowl beat eggs with electric mixer on high speed about 1 minute or till light and airy. Gradually add powdered sugar and beat on high speed about 15 minutes or till soft peaks form. Add oil of anise. Beat in flour mixture on low speed (dough will be thick). Cover tightly and let stand about 15 minutes for easier handling.

● Divide dough into thirds. Roll each into an 8-inch square. Let stand for 1 minute. Lightly dust a springerle rolling pin or mold with flour and roll or press into dough to make a clear design. With a sharp knife, cut cookies apart. Place on a lightly floured surface. Cover loosely with a towel and let stand overnight.

● Grease and sprinkle a cookie sheet with 1½ to 2 teaspoons crushed aniseed. Brush excess flour from cookies. With your finger, rub the bottom of each cookie lightly with cold water and place on the cookie sheet. Bake in a 300° oven about 20 minutes or till cookies are a light straw color. Remove and cool. Store cookies in a tightly covered container at least three days before eating. Makes 60 to 72.

Mincemeat Cornucopias

Tiny cream cheese pastries filled with orangy mincemeat.

1 cup butter *or* margarine
 1 8-ounce package cream
    cheese
½ cup sifted powdered sugar
 2 teaspoons finely shredded
    orange peel
 2 cups all-purpose flour
1¼ cups prepared mincemeat
 1 tablespoon orange juice

● Place butter or margarine and cream cheese in a large mixer bowl and let stand at room temperature about 30 minutes or till softened. Beat together butter and cream cheese. Add powdered sugar and beat till fluffy. Beat in *1 teaspoon* of the orange peel. Add flour and beat till well mixed. Cover and chill about 1 hour or till easy to handle.

● Roll dough ⅛ inch thick. Cut into rounds with a 2½-inch cookie cutter. Place on an ungreased cookie sheet. For filling, stir together mincemeat, orange juice, and remaining orange peel. Place about 1 teaspoon filling in the center of each round. Moisten the edge of the circle with a little water. Bring up two *adjacent* sides of dough and pinch to seal, forming a cornucopia. Bake in a 375° oven for 12 to 15 minutes or till done. Remove and cool. Makes about 48.

Apricot Fold-Overs

Tuck a whole brandied apricot inside each pastry pocket.

2 6-ounce packages dried
    apricots
½ cup apricot brandy
1½ cups all-purpose flour
¼ cup sugar
¼ teaspoon ground allspice
¾ cup butter *or* margarine
1 beaten egg yolk
⅓ cup dairy sour cream
    Apricot Brandy Icing

● Soak apricots in brandy about 1 hour or overnight. Drain and reserve brandy. Pat apricots dry.

● In a large mixing bowl combine flour, sugar, and allspice. Cut in butter till mixture resembles fine crumbs. Combine egg yolk and sour cream and stir into flour mixture till combined. Divide dough in half. Cover and chill several hours or overnight.

● Roll dough ⅛ inch thick. Cut into rounds with a 2½-inch cookie cutter. Place on an ungreased cookie sheet. Place one apricot on one half of each cookie. Fold over other half, leaving part of the apricot showing. Bake in a 350° oven about 12 minutes or till done. Remove and cool. Dip folded part of each cookie in Apricot Brandy Icing. Makes about 54.

Apricot Brandy Icing: Combine 1 cup sifted *powdered sugar* and 2 to 3 tablespoons of reserved *apricot brandy* to make icing of pouring consistency.

Honey-Wheat Cutouts

Honey and whole wheat are a natural combination in these thin crisps. They're delicious with or without a drizzle of icing.

1¼ cups whole wheat flour
¾ cup all-purpose flour
1 teaspoon ground coriander
½ teaspoon baking soda
¼ teaspoon salt
½ cup butter *or* margarine
⅔ cup packed brown sugar
1 egg
⅓ cup honey
1 teaspoon vanilla
    Vanilla Icing (see recipe,
      page 40)

● Stir together whole wheat flour, all-purpose flour, coriander, baking soda, and salt. In a large mixer bowl beat butter or margarine till softened. Add brown sugar and beat till fluffy. Add egg, honey, and vanilla and beat well. Add flour mixture and beat till well mixed. Divide dough in half. Cover and chill at least 2 hours or till easy to handle.

● On a well-floured surface roll dough ⅛ inch thick. Cut with cookie cutters. Place on a lightly greased cookie sheet. Bake in a 375° oven for 6 to 7 minutes or till done. Remove immediately and cool. If desired, drizzle with Vanilla Icing. Makes about 48.

Stags' Antlers

For a switch from typical holiday richness, serve these light, crisp Scandinavian favorites. Their shape is intended to resemble a deer's antlers.

2¼ cups all-purpose flour
½ cup cornstarch
½ teaspoon baking soda
½ teaspoon ground cardamom
¼ teaspoon salt
½ cup butter *or* margarine
¾ cup sugar
2 egg yolks
1 egg
¼ cup milk

● Stir together flour, cornstarch, baking soda, cardamom, and salt. In a large mixer bowl beat butter or margarine till softened. Add sugar and beat till fluffy. Beat in egg yolks and egg. Add milk and beat well. Gradually add flour mixture, beating till well mixed. Divide dough in half. Cover and chill several hours or till easy to handle.

● Roll each half of dough into a 12x6-inch rectangle. Cut each rectangle into thirty-six 2x1-inch strips. Place on an ungreased cookie sheet. On one long side of each strip, make a slit ¾ inch from each end, cutting slits a little more than halfway through strip. Curve to open slits. Sprinkle with additional sugar.

● Bake in a 350° oven for 10 to 12 minutes or till done. Remove and cool. Makes 72.

Cashew Crowns

Undercoated with chocolate, these cashew-laden shortbread cookies have an elegant look and a sophisticated flavor.

½ cup butter *or* margarine
⅓ cup sugar
1 egg
½ teaspoon vanilla
1 6¼-ounce can (1⅓ cups) cashews
1½ cups all-purpose flour
4 ounces (4 squares) semisweet chocolate, melted

● In a large mixer bowl beat butter or margarine till softened. Add sugar and beat till fluffy. Add egg and vanilla and beat well. Finely chop enough of the cashews to measure ½ cup. If remaining cashews are whole, split each in half lengthwise and reserve. Stir chopped cashews and flour into butter mixture.

● Roll dough ¼ inch thick. Cut into rounds with a 1¾-inch cookie cutter. Place on an ungreased cookie sheet and top each with one or two of the reserved cashew halves, pressing down gently. Bake in a 350° oven for 12 to 15 minutes or till done. Remove and cool.

● Spread the bottom of each with melted chocolate. Place, chocolate side up, on waxed paper till set. If desired, drizzle tops with chocolate. Makes about 30.

Wishing Cookies

When our Test Kitchen director discovered the wishing cookie tradition of her Swedish friends, she adapted the fun to one of her favorite cutout cookies.

3¼ cups all-purpose flour
1 teaspoon baking soda
1 teaspoon ground cinnamon
¾ teaspoon ground ginger
¼ teaspoon ground nutmeg
1 cup butter *or* margarine
1½ cups sugar
1 egg
2 tablespoons molasses
1 tablespoon water
½ teaspoon grated orange *or* lemon peel
Lace Icing

● Stir together flour, baking soda, cinnamon, ginger, and nutmeg. In a large mixer bowl beat butter or margarine till softened. Add sugar and beat till fluffy. Add egg, molasses, water, and peel and beat well. Gradually add flour mixture, beating till well mixed. Cover and chill about 2 hours or till easy to handle.

● Roll dough ⅛ inch thick. Cut with cookie cutters. Place on an ungreased cookie sheet. Bake in a 375° oven about 8 minutes or till done. Remove and cool. With a decorating bag and writing tip, pipe on a design with Lace Icing. Makes about 100.

Lace Icing: Stir together 2 cups sifted *powdered sugar,* ½ teaspoon *vanilla,* and enough *light cream or milk* (about 2 tablespoons) to make icing of piping consistency. If desired, tint with a few drops *food coloring.*

Making a wish
Place a cookie in the palm of your hand. Press in the center with one finger of your other hand. If the cookie breaks into three pieces and you can eat all three without saying a word, you get to make a wish. (Keeping quiet is the hard part!)

Italian Fig Cookies

Not a dainty cookie, this hearty fig-filled delight is the favorite of the editor on our staff with Italian heritage.

2½ cups all-purpose flour
⅓ cup sugar
¼ teaspoon baking powder
½ cup shortening
2 tablespoons butter *or* margarine
½ cup milk
1 beaten egg
1 8-ounce package (1½ cups) dried figs
¾ cup light raisins
¼ cup slivered almonds
¼ cup sugar
¼ cup hot water
¼ teaspoon ground cinnamon
Dash pepper
Confectioners' Glaze
Small multicolored decorative candies (optional)

● In a large mixing bowl combine flour, ⅓ cup sugar, and baking powder. Cut in shortening and butter or margarine till pieces are the size of small peas. Stir in the milk and egg till all is moistened. Divide dough in half. Cover and chill about 2 hours or till easy to handle.

● For filling, in a food processor bowl or with the coarse blade of a food grinder, process or grind figs, raisins, and almonds till coarsely chopped. In a medium mixing bowl combine the ¼ cup sugar, hot water, cinnamon, and pepper. Stir in the fruit mixture. Let filling stand till the dough is thoroughly chilled.

● Roll each half of the dough into a 12-inch square. Cut each square into twelve 4x3-inch rectangles. Using a heaping tablespoon of filling for each rectangle, spread filling along one of the short sides of the rectangle. Roll up from that side. Place rolls, seam side down, on an ungreased cookie sheet. Curve each roll slightly. Snip outer edge of curve three times.

● Bake in a 350° oven for 20 to 25 minutes or till done. Remove and cool. Spread with Confectioners' Glaze. Immediately sprinkle with decorative candies, if desired. Makes 24.

Confectioners' Glaze: Combine 1 cup sifted *powdered sugar* and ¼ teaspoon *vanilla*. Add enough *milk* (about 1 tablespoon) to make it spreadable.

Symbol Cookies

Cut out these traditional Hanukkah cookies to symbolize parts of Hebrew heritage such as the Lion of Judah and the menorah. You'll find special cutters at synagogue gift shops.

1½ cups all-purpose flour
1 teaspoon baking powder
1 teaspoon aniseed, crushed
½ cup pure vegetable shortening
½ cup sugar
1 egg yolk
¼ cup honey

● Stir together flour, baking powder, and aniseed. In a small mixer bowl beat shortening for 30 seconds. Add sugar and beat till fluffy. Add egg yolk and honey and beat well. Add flour mixture and beat till well mixed.

● Roll dough ¼ inch thick. Cut with cookie cutters. Place on a greased cookie sheet. Bake in a 375° oven for 6 to 7 minutes or till done. Cool on cookie sheet for 1 minute, then remove and cool thoroughly. Makes about 30.

BAR COOKIES

Trim time
from your busy schedule of
holiday preparations by
making fast and easy bar
cookies. Because you bake
the mixture all at once in a
pan and then cut it into
bars, you end up with lots of
cookies with a minimum
of effort.

Though bars are simple
to make, they're just as
inviting, and delicious, as
individually baked cookies.
From light and cakey to
rich and gooey, you'll find
your favorites here.

Using the Right Pan Size

Bar cookies are probably the easiest type of cookie to make with success, provided you use the size of pan stated in the recipe.

Bars baked in a pan that is too large will be thin and dry. A pan that is smaller than specified will give you bars that are underbaked.

Making Bars Level

Take extra care to level the unbaked mixture in the pan. Not only will the bars be more attractive, they will bake more evenly, too.

For batter-type bars, spread the batter evenly in the pan with a rubber scraper. Make sure it is about the same distance from the top of the pan on all sides and that the center is level with the edges.

For bars with a crumb or dough base, press the mixture into the pan with your hand so that it is the same thickness in all areas. Then, when spreading another mixture over the base, spread it evenly, as for batter-type bars.

When Are They Done?

To tell if cakelike bars are done, stick a wooden toothpick near the center of the uncut bars. If the toothpick comes out clean, they're ready.

For other types of bar cookies, such as filled or custard-type bars, specific doneness tests are provided in each recipe.

Cooling and Cutting Bars

Some bars need to be cut while still warm to prevent cracking or shattering. Others need to cool completely before cutting. Follow the directions for cooling given in the recipe.

Cool bars in the pan on a cooling rack. When cool, frost or sprinkle with powdered sugar, if you like. (Always frost *before* cutting to avoid having to frost bars one by one.)

Use a sharp knife to cut the pan of cookies into the size and shape bar you want. Remove a corner piece first, then the rest of the bars.

Carrot Bars

They're like tiny pieces of carrot cake, complete with cream cheese frosting.

⅓ cup butter *or* margarine
¼ cup water
1 cup all-purpose flour
1 cup sugar
1 teaspoon ground cinnamon
½ teaspoon baking soda
¼ teaspoon salt
¼ teaspoon ground nutmeg
¼ teaspoon ground ginger
1 slightly beaten egg
¼ cup buttermilk *or* sour milk*
½ teaspoon vanilla
1 cup shredded carrots
½ cup raisins
   Cinnamon Cream Cheese Frosting

● In a small saucepan combine butter and water. Bring to boiling, stirring to melt butter. Remove from heat and cool slightly.

● In a large mixing bowl stir together flour, sugar, cinnamon, baking soda, salt, nutmeg, and ginger. Add butter mixture, egg, buttermilk or sour milk, and vanilla and mix till combined. Fold in shredded carrots and raisins.

● Pour into a greased 13x9x2-inch baking pan. Bake in a 375° oven about 20 minutes or till done. Cool. Frost with Cinnamon Cream Cheese Frosting. Cut into bars. Makes 32.

Cinnamon Cream Cheese Frosting: In a small mixer bowl beat together one 3-ounce package *cream cheese,* ¼ cup *butter or margarine,* 1 teaspoon *vanilla,* and ¼ teaspoon ground *cinnamon* till light and fluffy. Gradually beat in 2 cups sifted *powdered sugar* till smooth.

*To make sour milk, combine ¾ teaspoon *lemon juice or vinegar* and enough *milk* to make ¼ cup. Let stand 5 minutes.

Maple-Coconut Bars

Chewy, buttery, and mildly maple.

¾ cup all-purpose flour
½ teaspoon baking powder
¼ teaspoon salt
1 4-ounce can (1⅓ cups) shredded coconut
¼ cup butter *or* margarine
¾ cup sugar
1 egg
½ teaspoon maple flavoring
¼ cup chopped walnuts
1 tablespoon butter *or* margarine, melted

● Stir together flour, baking powder, and salt. Reserve ½ *cup* of the coconut for topping and finely chop the remainder.

● In a small mixer bowl beat ¼ cup butter or margarine till softened. Add sugar and beat till well combined. Add egg and maple flavoring and beat just till combined.

● Add flour mixture and beat till well mixed. Stir in the finely chopped coconut and the nuts. Spread in a greased 8x8x2-inch baking pan.

● Combine reserved ½ cup coconut and 1 tablespoon melted butter and sprinkle over mixture in pan. Bake in a 350° oven about 30 minutes or till done. Cool. Cut into bars. Makes 24.

Fruitcake Squares

A rich fruitcake concoction tops a buttery crumb crust.

⅓ cup butter *or* margarine
1 12-ounce box vanilla wafers, finely crushed (3¼ cups)
1 cup pecan halves
¾ cup chopped dates
¾ cup halved green candied cherries
¾ cup halved red candied cherries
½ cup chopped candied pineapple
1 14-ounce can (1¼ cups) *sweetened condensed milk*
¼ cup bourbon *or* milk

● In a small saucepan melt butter or margarine, then pour into a 15x10x1-inch baking pan, tilting pan to spread butter evenly. Sprinkle crushed vanilla wafers evenly over butter in pan. Arrange nuts, dates, and candied fruits evenly over the crumb mixture and press down gently.

● Combine sweetened condensed milk and bourbon or milk and pour evenly over top. Bake in a 350° oven for 20 to 25 minutes or till set. Cool. Cut into squares. Makes 60.

Mocha Cinnamon Fingers

After baking, sprinkle the warm coffee-flavored base with chocolate pieces and, when softened, spread them into a thin glossy sheet.

2 teaspoons instant coffee crystals
½ teaspoon water
½ teaspoon vanilla
2 cups all-purpose flour
1 teaspoon ground cinnamon
1 cup butter *or* margarine
½ cup sugar
½ cup packed brown sugar
1 egg yolk
1 6-ounce package (1 cup) semisweet chocolate pieces
1 cup finely chopped walnuts *or* pecans

● In a small bowl stir together coffee crystals, water, and vanilla till coffee crystals are dissolved. In a medium bowl stir together flour and cinnamon.

● In a large mixer bowl beat butter or margarine till softened. Add sugar and brown sugar and beat till fluffy. Add egg yolk and coffee mixture and beat well. Gradually add flour mixture, beating till well mixed. Press evenly into an ungreased 15x10x1-inch baking pan.

● Bake in a 350° oven for 15 to 18 minutes or till done. Immediately sprinkle chocolate pieces over top. Let stand till chocolate is softened, then spread evenly. Sprinkle with nuts. Cut into bars while warm. Cool. Makes 48.

Fruitcake
Squares

Mocha Cinnamon
Fingers

Grasshopper
Cheesecake Bars
(see recipe, page 62)

Grasshopper Cheesecake Bars

Mint-flavored cheesecake separates two layers of chocolate crumbs. (Pictured on page 61.)

1   8-ounce package cream
    cheese
¾   cup all-purpose flour
⅓   cup sugar
⅓   cup unsweetened
    cocoa powder
6   tablespoons butter *or*
    margarine
¼   cup sugar
1   egg
½   teaspoon peppermint
    extract
4   *or* 5 drops green food
    coloring
¼   cup milk

● Place cream cheese in a small mixer bowl and let stand at room temperature about 30 minutes or till softened.

● Stir together flour, ⅓ cup sugar, and cocoa powder. Cut in butter or margarine till mixture resembles fine crumbs. Set aside 1 cup of the mixture for topping. Press remaining mixture onto the bottom of an ungreased 8x8x2-inch baking pan. Bake in a 350° oven for 15 minutes.

● Meanwhile, beat together softened cream cheese and ¼ cup sugar till fluffy. Add egg, peppermint extract, and food coloring and beat well. Stir in milk. Spread over baked layer.

● Sprinkle top with reserved crumbs. Return to the 350° oven and bake for 20 to 25 minutes or till done. Cool. Cut into bars. Chill to store. Makes 25.

Pumpkin-Chocolate Chip Bars

Scatter a cinnamon-sugar mixture over the batter before baking.

2   cups all-purpose flour
2   teaspoons baking powder
2   teaspoons ground cinnamon
1   teaspoon baking soda
1   teaspoon salt
4   beaten eggs
1   16-ounce can pumpkin
1½ cups sugar
¼   cup cooking oil
1   6-ounce package (1 cup)
    semisweet chocolate
    pieces
3   tablespoons sugar
½   teaspoon ground cinnamon

● Stir together flour, baking powder, 2 teaspoons cinnamon, baking soda, and salt. In a medium mixing bowl combine eggs, pumpkin, 1½ cups sugar, and oil. Add flour mixture and mix just till moistened. Stir in chocolate pieces.

● Spread in an ungreased 15x10x1-inch baking pan. Stir together 3 tablespoons sugar and ½ teaspoon cinnamon and sprinkle evenly over batter. Bake in a 350° oven for 25 to 30 minutes or till done. Cool. Cut into bars. Makes 36.

Scandinavian Almond Bars

This unique recipe from one editor's Norwegian grandmother has become a favorite of many of us. (Pictured on pages 6 and 68.)

1¾ cups all-purpose flour
  2 teaspoons baking powder
  ¼ teaspoon salt
  ½ cup butter *or* margarine
  1 cup sugar
  1 egg
  ½ teaspoon almond extract
     Milk
  ½ cup sliced almonds,
        coarsely chopped
     Almond Icing

● Stir together flour, baking powder, and salt. In a large mixer bowl beat butter or margarine till softened. Add sugar and beat till fluffy. Add egg and almond extract and beat well. Add flour mixture and beat till well mixed.

● Divide dough into fourths. Form each into a 12-inch roll. Place two rolls 4 to 5 inches apart on an ungreased cookie sheet. Flatten till 3 inches wide. Repeat with remaining rolls.

● Brush flattened rolls with milk and sprinkle with almonds. Bake in a 325° oven for 12 to 14 minutes or till edges are lightly browned. While cookies are still warm, cut them crosswise at a diagonal into 1-inch strips. Cool. Drizzle with Almond Icing. Makes 48.

Almond Icing: Stir together 1 cup sifted *powdered sugar,* ¼ teaspoon *almond extract,* and enough *milk* (3 to 4 teaspoons) to make icing of drizzling consistency.

Cutting the bars
While the bars are still warm and soft on the cookie sheet, use a sharp knife to cut the baked dough diagonally into 1-inch strips. Cool the strips on a wire rack before drizzling with icing.

Pan Lebkuchen

This easy bake-in-the-pan version of the German cutout cookie retains the traditional flavors of honey, spices, candied fruits, and nuts. (Pictured on the cover.)

2 cups all-purpose flour
1 tablespoon pumpkin pie spice
½ teaspoon baking soda
1 egg
2 tablespoons cooking oil
½ cup packed brown sugar
⅓ cup honey
⅓ cup dark molasses
½ cup chopped almonds
½ cup diced mixed candied fruits and peels, finely chopped
Lemon Icing
Additional diced mixed candied fruits and peels

● Stir together flour, pumpkin pie spice, and baking soda. In a large mixer bowl beat together egg and oil. Add brown sugar and beat till fluffy. Stir in honey and molasses. Add flour mixture and beat till well mixed. Stir in chopped almonds and candied fruits and peels.

● Spread in a greased 15x10x1-inch baking pan. Bake in a 350° oven for 15 to 20 minutes or till done. Immediately score into bars with a sharp knife. Brush on Lemon Icing. Garnish each bar with additional candied fruit. Cool thoroughly. Cut into bars. Makes 32.

Lemon Icing: In a small mixer bowl beat together 1 *egg white*, 1½ cups sifted *powdered sugar*, ½ teaspoon finely shredded *lemon peel*, and 1 tablespoon *lemon juice* till smooth.

Date Bars

Rolled oats in the base and topping give the bars an old-fashioned, toasty flavor.

1 8-ounce package (1⅓ cups) pitted whole dates, snipped
¾ cup water
2 tablespoons sugar
1 teaspoon vanilla
1½ cups all-purpose flour
1½ cups quick-cooking rolled oats
¾ cup packed brown sugar
½ teaspoon baking soda
¼ teaspoon ground cinnamon
¾ cup butter *or* margarine

● For filling, in a saucepan combine dates, water, and sugar. Cook and stir over medium heat till bubbly. Cook and stir for 4 to 5 minutes more or till thickened. Remove from heat. Stir in vanilla and cool.

● Combine flour, oats, brown sugar, baking soda, and cinnamon. Cut in butter or margarine till mixture is crumbly. Press *three-fourths* of the crumbs onto the bottom of an ungreased 13x9x2-inch baking pan. Spread filling over crumbs. Sprinkle with remaining crumbs. Bake in a 375° oven for 25 to 30 minutes or till crumbs are golden. Cool. Cut into bars. Makes 32.

Score warm Pan Lebkuchen before icing and decorating.

1 Scoring into bars
While the lebkuchen is still warm in the pan, use a sharp knife to score it into bars, cutting just through the top crust. Scoring helps to define the shape of the bars so that after they're iced, you will be able to see the outline of each bar, making decorating easier.

2 Decorating the bars
Brush the icing over the scored bars. Cut and arrange pieces of candied fruit on the bars, using your creativity to give each a unique design. Once the bars are thoroughly cooled, cut through completely at the score marks to separate them.

Apple Butter Bars

Tender and cakelike, with bits of dried apricots, peaches, apples, and raisins throughout.

1	6-ounce package (1½ cups) mixed dried fruit bits
1½	cups all-purpose flour
½	teaspoon baking soda
½	teaspoon ground cinnamon
¼	teaspoon salt
½	cup butter *or* margarine
¾	cup packed brown sugar
2	eggs
½	cup apple butter
	Powdered sugar

● Pour enough *boiling water* over fruit bits to cover, then let stand 5 minutes. Drain.

● Meanwhile, stir together flour, baking soda, cinnamon, and salt. In a large mixer bowl beat butter or margarine till softened. Add brown sugar and beat till fluffy. Add eggs and apple butter and beat well. Add flour mixture and beat till well mixed.

● Stir in drained fruit. Spread in a greased 13x9x2-inch baking pan. Bake in a 350° oven for 25 to 30 minutes or till done. Cool. Sift powdered sugar over cookies. Cut into bars. Makes 36.

Chewy Raisin Bars

Mix the no-fuss batter in a saucepan.

½	cup packed brown sugar
⅓	cup butter *or* margarine
½	cup all-purpose flour
¼	teaspoon baking powder
1	egg
1	teaspoon vanilla
¾	cup raisins
¼	cup chopped walnuts
	Powdered sugar

● In a saucepan heat and stir brown sugar and butter or margarine till butter is melted. Remove from the heat and cool about 5 minutes. Meanwhile, stir together flour and baking powder.

● Beat egg and vanilla into mixture in the saucepan till well mixed. Stir in flour mixture. Stir in raisins and walnuts. Spread in a greased 8x8x2-inch baking pan. Bake in a 350° oven about 25 minutes or till done. Cut into bars while warm. Cool. Sift powdered sugar over bars before serving. Makes 24.

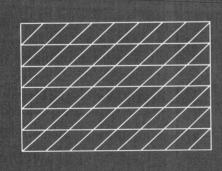

Cutting Bars Into Triangles And Diamonds

Add a festive look to a plate of cookies by cutting bars into unusual shapes.

● To make triangles, simply cut bars into squares and halve them diagonally.

● To make diamonds, first make straight parallel cuts 1 to 1½ inches apart down the length of the pan. Then make diagonal cuts as shown, keeping the lines as even as possible. You will have irregularly shaped pieces at each end of the pan that you can use to fill in small gaps on the holiday cookie platter.

Spiced Gooey Bars

A great-tasting hodgepodge of graham crackers, chocolate, raisins, spices, and nuts.

⅔ cup butter *or* margarine

2¼ cups finely crushed graham crackers (about 32 squares)

2 teaspoons ground cinnamon

½ teaspoon ground allspice

1 cup chopped walnuts *or* pecans

½ cup raisins

1 6-ounce package (1 cup) semisweet chocolate pieces

1 14-ounce can (1¼ cups) *sweetened condensed milk*

● In a medium saucepan melt butter or margarine. Remove from the heat. Combine crushed graham crackers, cinnamon, and allspice, then stir into melted butter in saucepan. Press *two-thirds* of the crumb mixture evenly onto the bottom of an ungreased 13x9x2-inch baking pan.

● Layer, in order, nuts, raisins, and chocolate pieces. Pour sweetened condensed milk evenly over all. Sprinkle with remaining crumb mixture.

● Bake in a 350° oven about 30 minutes or till golden brown and edges are firm. Cool. Cut into bars. Makes 36.

Lemon Squares

Once a fad recipe, it still ranks high on the most-wanted list.

6 tablespoons butter *or* margarine

¼ cup sugar

¼ teaspoon salt

1 cup all-purpose flour

2 eggs

¾ cup sugar

2 tablespoons all-purpose flour

¼ teaspoon finely shredded lemon peel

3 tablespoons lemon juice

¼ teaspoon baking powder
Powdered sugar (optional)

● In a small mixer bowl beat butter or margarine till softened. Add ¼ cup sugar and salt and beat till fluffy. Stir in 1 cup flour. Press dough onto the bottom of a greased 8x8x2-inch baking pan. Bake in a 350° oven for 15 minutes.

● Meanwhile, in the mixer bowl beat eggs. Add ¾ cup sugar, 2 tablespoons flour, lemon peel, lemon juice, and baking powder. Beat about 3 minutes or till slightly thickened. Pour the lemon mixture over the baked layer.

● Return to the 350° oven and bake for 25 to 30 minutes or till edges are light golden brown and center is set. Cool. If desired, sift powdered sugar over cookies. Cut into squares. Makes 16.

Jam-Filled Crumb Bars

Rocky Road Brownies

Scandinavian Almond Bars
(see recipe, page 63)

Rocky Road Brownies

Marshmallows, chocolate, and nuts on top of these moist brownies account for their name.

1 6-ounce package (1 cup) semisweet chocolate pieces
1 cup all-purpose flour
½ teaspoon baking powder
⅓ cup butter *or* margarine
¾ cup sugar
2 eggs
1 teaspoon vanilla
¼ cup chopped nuts
½ cup tiny marshmallows

● In a heavy small saucepan heat and stir *½ cup* of the chocolate pieces over low heat till melted. Remove from heat and cool slightly. Meanwhile, stir together flour and baking powder.

● In a small mixer bowl beat butter or margarine till softened. Add sugar and beat till well combined. Add eggs and vanilla and beat well. Beat in melted chocolate. Add flour mixture and beat till well mixed. Spread in a greased 9x9x2-inch baking pan.

● Bake in a 350° oven for 20 minutes. On baked base, layer remaining chocolate pieces, nuts, and marshmallows. Bake 5 to 10 minutes more or till marshmallows are golden. Cool. Cut into bars. Makes 24.

Jam-Filled Crumb Bars

Make three different bars at once by using all three kinds of jam.

1¾ cups all-purpose flour
½ cup finely chopped nuts
¾ cup butter *or* margarine
½ cup sifted powdered sugar
¼ teaspoon finely shredded lemon peel
¾ cup blackberry jam, apricot preserves, *or* red raspberry preserves
1 tablespoon all-purpose flour

● Stir together 1¾ cups flour and the finely chopped nuts. In a large mixer bowl beat butter or margarine till softened. Add powdered sugar and lemon peel and beat till fluffy. Add flour mixture and beat till crumbly.

● Press *two-thirds* of the crumbs onto the bottom of an ungreased 9x9x2-inch baking pan. Spread with one kind of jam. (Or, using ¼ cup each of the three kinds of jam, spread a 3-inch-wide strip of each on crumb base.) Stir 1 tablespoon flour into remaining crumb mixture and sprinkle over jam.

● Bake in a 375° oven for 25 to 30 minutes or till crumbs are golden. Cool. Cut into bars. Makes 24.

Praline Bars

Lots and lots of pecans!

1¾ cups all-purpose flour
⅓ cup packed brown sugar
1 teaspoon baking powder
½ teaspoon salt
¾ cup butter *or* margarine
2 eggs
4 tablespoons praline liqueur
    or brandy
2 cups sifted powdered sugar
2 cups finely chopped pecans
36 pecan halves

● For dough, in a large mixing bowl stir together flour, brown sugar, baking powder, and salt. Cut in butter or margarine till mixture is crumbly. Beat together *one* of the eggs and *2 tablespoons* of the liqueur and stir into flour mixture. Press into a greased 13x9x2-inch baking pan.

● In a small mixing bowl combine remaining egg and liqueur. Mix in powdered sugar. Stir in chopped nuts and spread over dough. Arrange pecan halves on top in six rows of six each.

● Bake in a 375° oven about 25 minutes or till set. Cut into bars while warm. Cool. Makes 36.

Chocolate Pecan-Pie Bars

Similar to pecan pie only we put the pecans in the crust and added chocolate to the filling!

1¼ cups all-purpose flour
¼ cup sugar
½ teaspoon baking powder
½ teaspoon ground cinnamon
½ cup butter *or* margarine
1 cup finely chopped pecans
¼ cup butter *or* margarine
1 square (1 ounce) semisweet
    chocolate
3 eggs
1¼ cups packed brown sugar
2 tablespoons bourbon *or*
    water
1 teaspoon vanilla

● For crust, in a medium mixing bowl stir together flour, sugar, baking powder, and cinnamon. Cut in ½ cup butter or margarine till mixture resembles coarse crumbs. Stir in pecans. Press onto the bottom of an ungreased 13x9x2-inch baking pan. Bake in a 350° oven for 10 minutes.

● Meanwhile, in a heavy small saucepan heat ¼ cup butter or margarine and chocolate over low heat till melted, stirring occasionally. Remove from the heat and cool slightly.

● In a small mixing bowl beat eggs. Add brown sugar, bourbon or water, vanilla, and the chocolate mixture and beat well. Pour over baked crust. Return to the 350° oven and bake about 20 minutes or till set. Cool. Cut into bars. Makes 36.

DROP COOKIES

Drop cookies are named for the way they're formed on the cookie sheet. The soft dough drops from spoon to cookie sheet in mounds that spread when baked. The cookies may be cakey or chewy, plain or brimming with chunks of nuts, fruit, or chocolate.

Some, such as Fudge Ecstasies, need no embellishment at all. The name speaks for itself. Others, you may want to fancy up with a little frosting or an icing drizzle.

Trixie **realized**

something.

Trixie turned to her daddy and said,

"Now, please don't get fussy,"
said her daddy.

Well, she had no choice....

Trixie bawled.

She went boneless.

She did everything she could to show how unhappy she was.

By the time they got
home, her daddy was
unhappy, too.

As soon as Trixie's mommy opened the door, she asked,

The whole family ran down the block.

And they ran through the park.

They zoomed past the school,

and into the Laundromat.

Trixie's daddy looked for Knuffle Bunny.

And looked . . .

and looked . . .

and looked . . .

But Knuffle Bunny was
nowhere to be found. . . .

So Trixie's daddy
decided to look harder.

Until . . .

And those were the first words Trixie ever said.

This book is dedicated to
the real Trixie and her mommy.
Special thanks to
Anne and Alessandra;
Noah, Megan, and Edward;
the 358 6th Avenue Laundromat;
and my neighbors in Park Slope, Brooklyn.

-Mo